massage
basics

Photographs by Alberto Bertoldi and Mario Matteucci

Graphic design and layout by
Paola Masera and Amelia Verga
with Beatrice Brancaccio

Translation by Chiara Tarsia

Library of Congress Cataloging-in-Publication Data

10 9 8 7 6 5 4 3 2

Published by Sterling Publishing Co., Inc.
387 Park Avenue South, New York, N.Y. 10016
Originally published in Italy under the title *Massagio* and
©1997 by R.C.S. Libri S.p.A.
English translation © 1998 by Sterling Publishing Company, Inc.
Distributed in Canada by Sterling Publishing
C/oCanadian Manda Group, One Atlantic Avenue, Suite 105
Toronto, Ontario, Canada M6K 3E7
Distributed in Great Britain by Chrysalis Books Group PLC,
The Chrysalis Building, Bramley Road, London W10 6SP, England
Distributed in Australia by Capricorn Link (Australia) Pty Ltd.
P.O. Box 704, Windsor, NSW 2756 Australia
Printed in China

ISBN 1-4027-1172-7

massage
basics

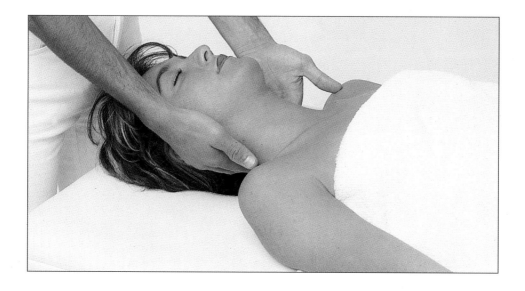

Davide Sechi

Main Street
A division of Sterling Publishing Co., Inc.
New York

TABLE OF CONTENTS

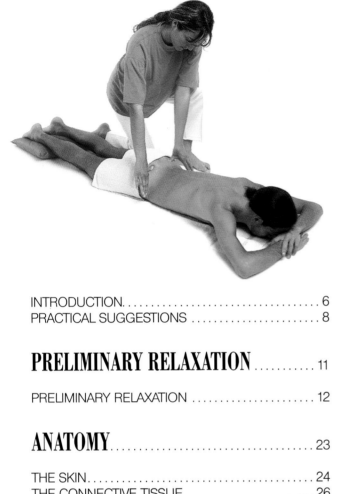

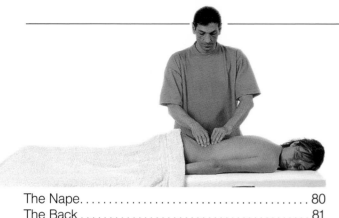

TO EACH HIS OWN...

MASSAGE AND AROMATHERAPY

GLOSSARY

INDEX

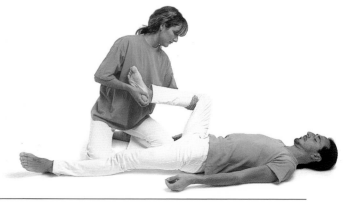

INTRODUCTION

Written simply but scientifically, this book makes human anatomy and physiology accessible even to a novice and shows the hows and whys of basic massage techniques. Professional practitioners may also gain important insights from studying this handbook, because it can help to bring a moment of reflection, a way to check on one's own activity, and even a possibility for self-appraisal, confrontation, and personal growth.

I would suggest that beginners follow the order in which the book is laid out and practice one particular technique at a time. The best results can be obtained by practicing with an equally enthusiastic friend and switching the roles of the person massaging and the person being massaged. Read each chapter carefully, gleaning an understanding of which organs are to be worked on, the effects to be obtained, and why. Look at the pictures and captions, then read the complete explanation of the technique to be used. Now you and your companion should try out the technique on each other, exchanging your impressions about the results. Repeat each technique several times until you feel confident. Always note your partner's reactions following a massage and check that this agrees with those

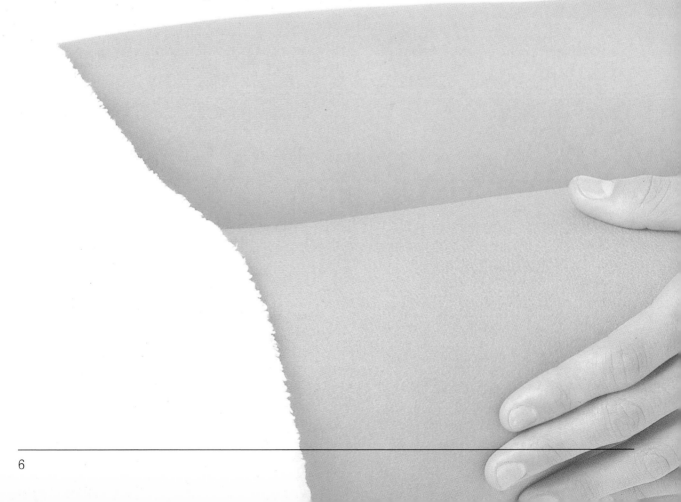

described in the manual. But remember, before beginning any technique, go over all the notes regarding endangerments. Always make sure that the person you are about to treat fits the description given of those people who are safe to be massaged. When in doubt, it is best to postpone the treatment and consult a doctor who will know best how to proceed. It is important to remember that your intervention can never replace that of a doctor, the only person in a position to make a diagnosis and prescribe an appropriate treatment.

In the first part of the book, the Western orientation to massage is represented, and in it I describe the theory and practice of Swedish massage, manual lymphatic drainage, and connective tissue massage. The second part of the book draws on both Eastern and Western traditions, focusing on foot reflexology, Shiatsu (both of which originated in the East), and a mixed technique which is very effective for stress.

Each chapter on a specific technique is comprised as follows: a theoretical section covering anatomical and physiological elements of the tissues involved (essential for pinpointing the areas to be worked on as well as all possible reactions); a practical section which explains the massage techniques in detail and indicates the mistakes to be avoided; a summary of the technique, with notes on the advisability of the massage, along with some final considerations.

Since the back offers a wide and flat surface which is easy to work on, this is the area where you begin learning each technique, but, where appropriate, variations in technique required for treatment of other parts of the body are given.

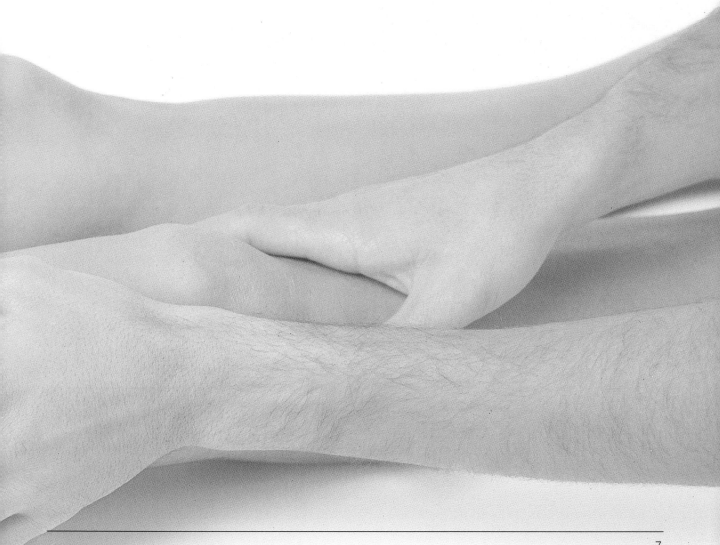

PRACTICAL SUGGESTIONS

The term "massage" comes from the Arab *mass* meaning "to touch" or "to feel," and this type of treatment is a basic to physical therapy. Physical therapy is a branch of rehabilitating medicine that makes use of all forms of mechanical, electrical, thermal, chemical, and radioactive energy for therapeutic purposes. In massage, a practitioner uses mechanical heat in particular on the body's tissues in order to trigger beneficial reactions in the body mainly through its reflex reactions. The extent and type of physiological reaction in the cells, tissues, and organs depends on the duration of the stimulus and on the degree of force, swiftness, and rhythm of the treatment.

Massage is an art that demands technical, physiological, and emotional involvement. Technique may be learned, and you will learn it through this book, but the other two factors are personal qualities and derive from individual enthusiasm and style. Practice and experience will help increase and improve these qualities in you.

It must always be remembered that your partner, on feeling the sensation of your touch, may assume a state of defense, a natural biological reaction caused by new stimuli. It is up to you to reassure your partner, encouraging a more relaxed state. Therefore a feeling of mutual sympathy must be established, one that will allow your partner to relax completely into your friendly hands. If you are not aware of your partner's personal reaction to you, you will never make a good practitioner.

The old adage "if it hurts it's doing good" has had its day. In fact, whoever provokes pain while massaging is not working correctly from a technical point of view. Massage can be applied even on sore areas without causing pain and should result in the patient's feeling rather like having awoken from refreshing sleep, with a deep sense of well-being.

The patient's reactions must be received and responded to in order for a massage to have its full therapeutic effect, because the treatment is more

than a mechanical application of hands. In order to carry out a massage properly and satisfactorily, the following general suggestions should be followed:
- Adopt those manipulations that produce pleasant sensations and reject those not welcomed. You can perceive which these are through an unspoken or spoken dialogue with your partner. Remember, it is the agility and elasticity of the hands rather than muscular force that is important.
- Make sure your position is comfortable for you and that you are able to stay balanced for all the movements you need to make.
- Wear practical, uncluttered clothes. Converse with discretion in subdued tones, without exaggeration or confidential attitudes. The practitioner, while seen as a friend, must take on a more formal role.
- Start the treatment with light movements, suitable for the first approach with a new human personality. Introduce yourself by beginning each massage with stroking motions. Exit from a session in the same way.
- Carry out the massage with a calm, predictable rhythm, applying special care to sore areas, and avoiding possible areas of infection and bruises.
- End the massage with movements that become gradually slower, lighter, and gentler, avoiding a sudden stop which could interrupt the state of relaxation.
- When possible, cover your partner at the end of the treatment and allow a resting period for a few minutes, as this allows the body to integrate the new physiological information.

SURROUNDINGS

The surroundings should be airy, spacious, hygenic, and welcoming, and give an impression of order. and efficiency. Temperature should be kept around 23 °C, and it is a good idea to have a light cotton sheet and perhaps a blanket handy to cover parts of the body not being massaged. Soft, suffused lighting is advisable and direct rays should never be trained on the face. A musical background is favored by many practitioners, while others opt for silence. The choice depends on you and your partner's preference. The market offers numerous creams, oils, talcs, and so forth suitable for massage. Choose the ones you prefer, in agreement with your partner, and use just enough to limit friction.
- Avoid spreading the product directly on the partner's body, but warm and spread the substance first in your hands. Avoid mineral oils as they do not allow the skin to breathe. Also make sure you are not using a product to which your patient may be allergic: for example, some people react badly to almond and/or wheat germ oils.

OVERALL ADVICE

Massage is advisable:
- in the presence of general, physical, and psychic fatigue, as it helps give tone to body and spirit alike. In fact, it stimulates that sense of well-being on which a healthy neurophysical condition depends;
- in cases of prolonged inactivity;
- in cases of reduced muscular tone and tropism.

SPECIFIC ADVICE

Adopt one of the following methods according to need:
- relaxing massage: suitable for those interested in maintaining their physical appearance and a sense of well-being;
- therapeutic massage: suitable where there exists damage due to trauma or surgical operations, particularly orthopedic; degenerative disorders such as arthritis; damage to the peripheral nervous system;
- sport massage for athletes, practiced before a competition (stimulating) or after a competition (relaxing).

WHEN NOT ADVISABLE

Swedish massage is never recommended where there are:
- diseases of the cardiovascular and respiratory systems with inflammation or infection;
- recent traumatic lesions such as bruises, sprains, or fractures, because it may cause a worsening of the situation or may interfere with the healing process;
- varicose veins, fragile capillary vessels, phlebitis;
- sores;
- a febrile state;
- persons with serious personality problems.

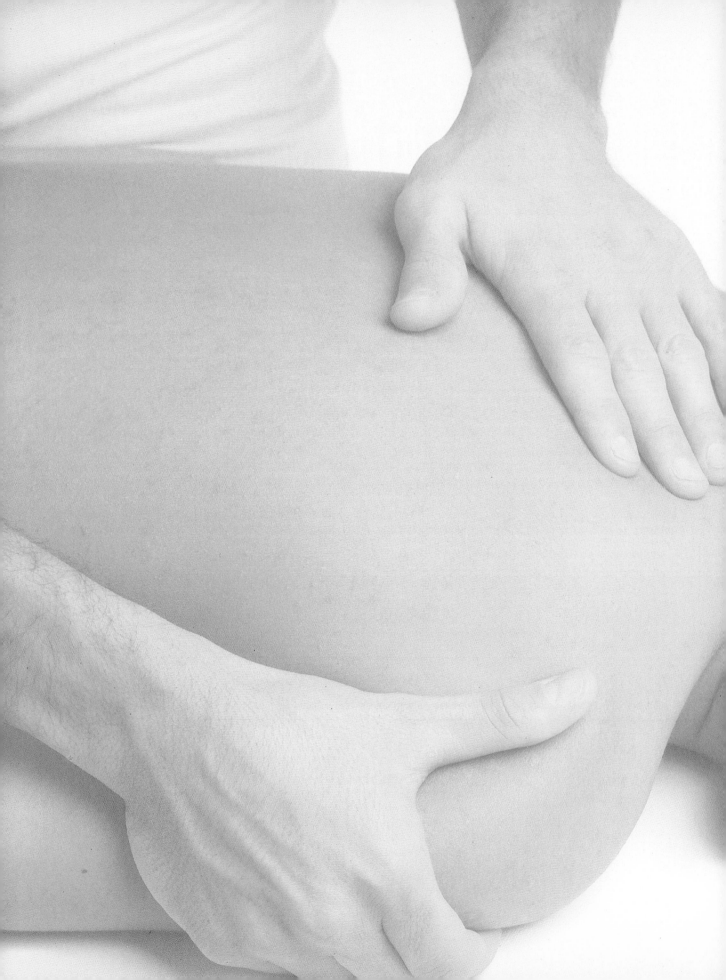

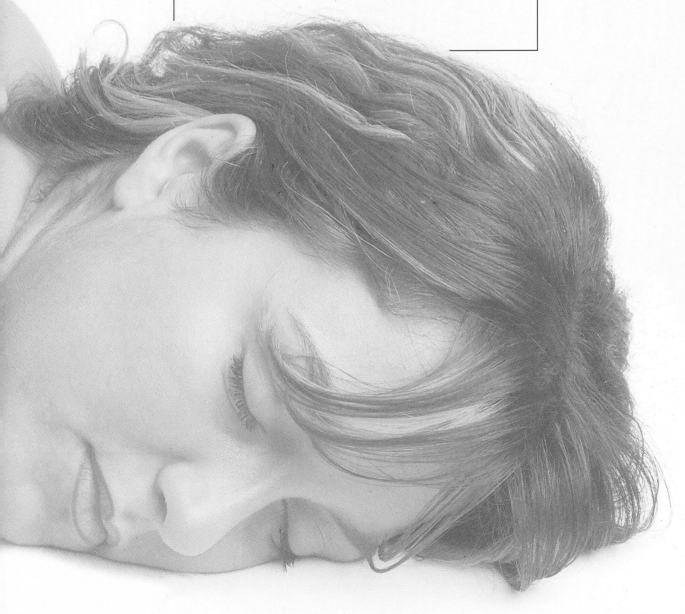

PRELIMINARY RELAXATION

PRELIMINARY RELAXATION

A special relaxing treatment is not always required before the massage proper, but when the patient is hypertense, it can be useful for breaking the ice and making initial body contact. The preliminary treatment should last about 30 minutes, but if time is short, fewer manipulations will be sufficient.

Your partner stretches out on a mattress or folded blanket. Try to synchronize your breathing with your partner's before starting. Each of the manipulations should be carried out in the same way on both the right and left sides.

1 *Kneeling at your partner's feet, grasp the foot and give several small thrusts forward, using your own body to transmit the movements along your partner's whole body.*

2 *Same hold as in the preceding exercise. With quick, slight flips of your wrist, make the legs rotate on their axis.*

3 *Turn both of the legs inwards, then outwards, then release them.*

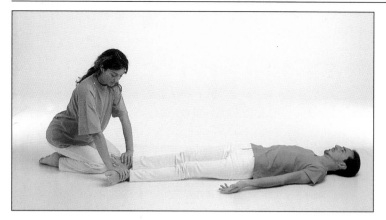

4 *Turn one leg outwards, the other inwards, and vice versa.*

5 *Grasp a foot and stretch the leg gradually by leaning backwards. Perform the stretch as your partner exhales.*

6 *Gradually stretch both legs together, proceeding as in the previous exercise.*

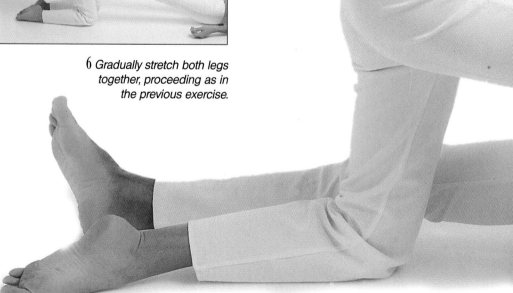

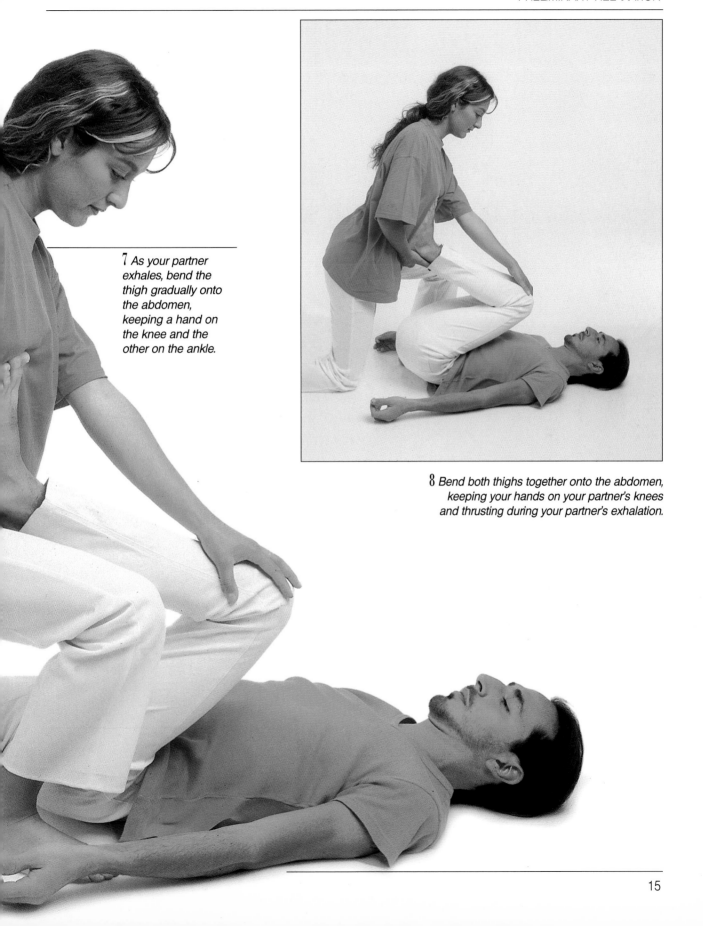

7 As your partner exhales, bend the thigh gradually onto the abdomen, keeping a hand on the knee and the other on the ankle.

8 Bend both thighs together onto the abdomen, keeping your hands on your partner's knees and thrusting during your partner's exhalation.

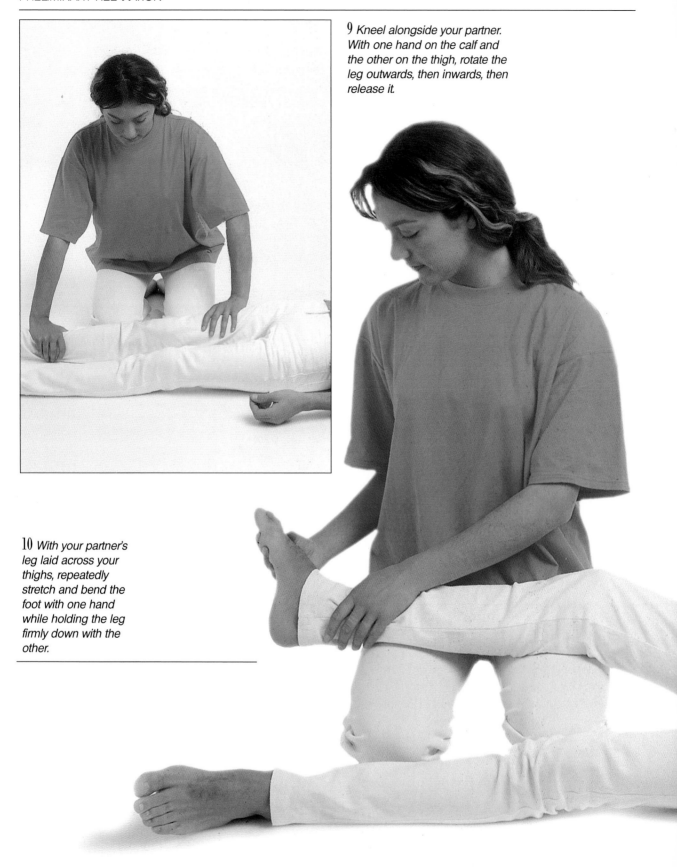

9 *Kneel alongside your partner. With one hand on the calf and the other on the thigh, rotate the leg outwards, then inwards, then release it.*

10 *With your partner's leg laid across your thighs, repeatedly stretch and bend the foot with one hand while holding the leg firmly down with the other.*

11 *Proceed as in exercise 10, stretching and bending the foot,*

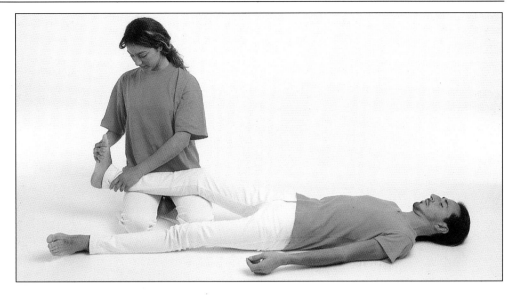

and add sideways and circular movements of the ankle.

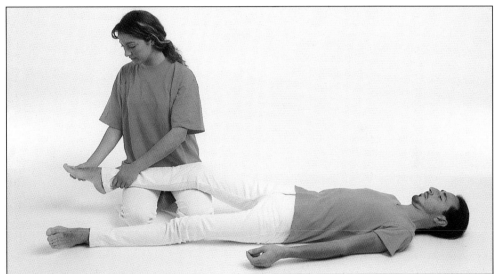

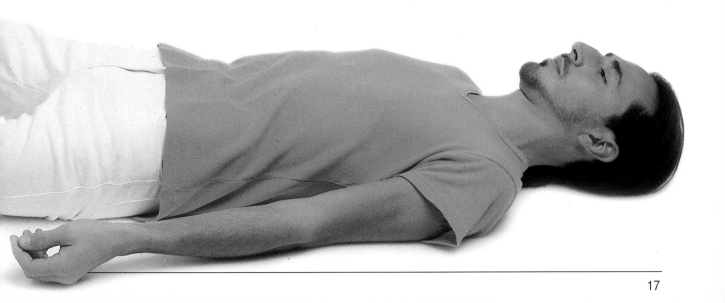

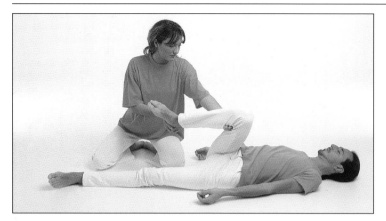

12 *Using both hands, bend the partner's knee so as to move the hip slowly and gradually in all directions.*

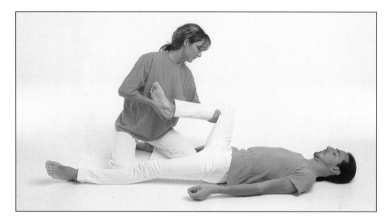

Along with the flexing movements, make the hip move in a circle, both clockwise and counterclockwise.

13 *Bend the partner's leg, with the foot well-placed on the ground. Hold the ankle fast with one hand. By inserting your arm under the knee, perform short traction movements of the leg.*

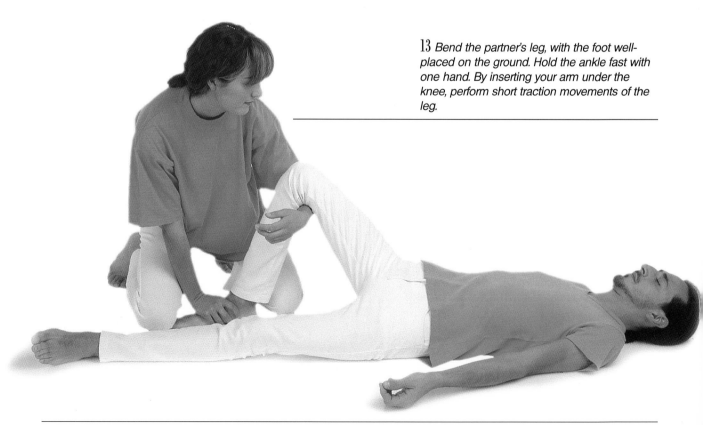

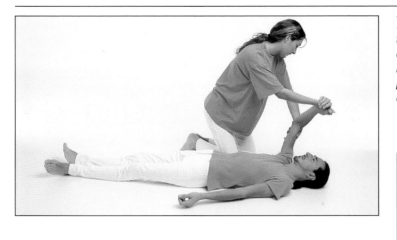

14 *Kneel by the partner's shoulder. Grasp the thumb and circulate the arm and shoulder in all directions, at all possible levels. Just as with the leg, all the movements may be combined to produce circular motions both clockwise and counterclockwise.*

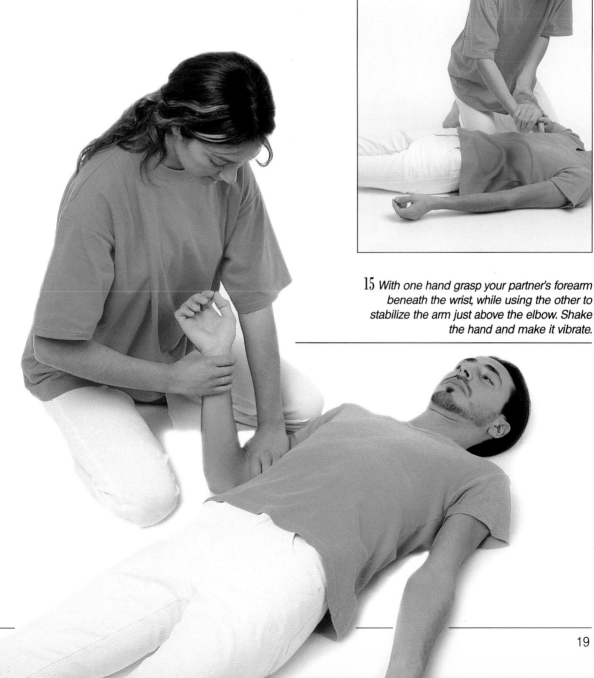

15 *With one hand grasp your partner's forearm beneath the wrist, while using the other to stabilize the arm just above the elbow. Shake the hand and make it vibrate.*

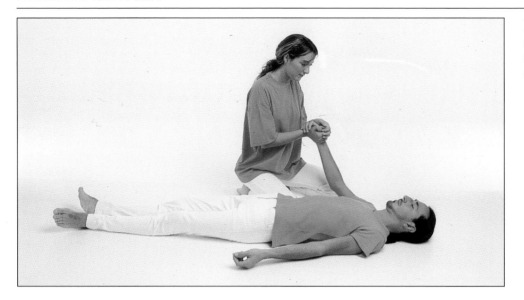

16 *Clasp the partner's hands in yours and shake the partner's arm.*

17 *During your partner's inhalation, gently stretch the arm upwards. Then on the exhalation, relax the stretch.*

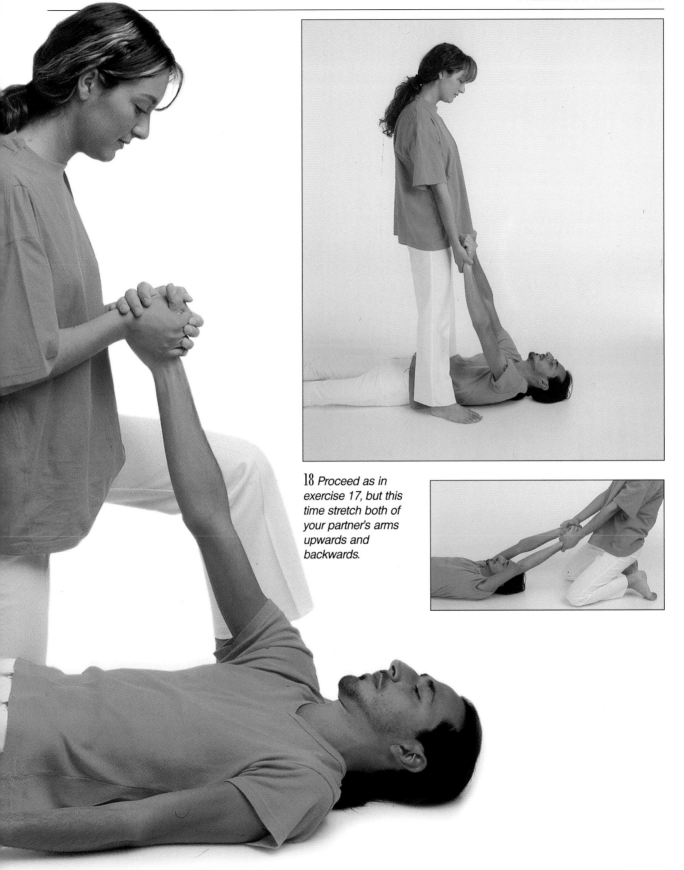

18 *Proceed as in exercise 17, but this time stretch both of your partner's arms upwards and backwards.*

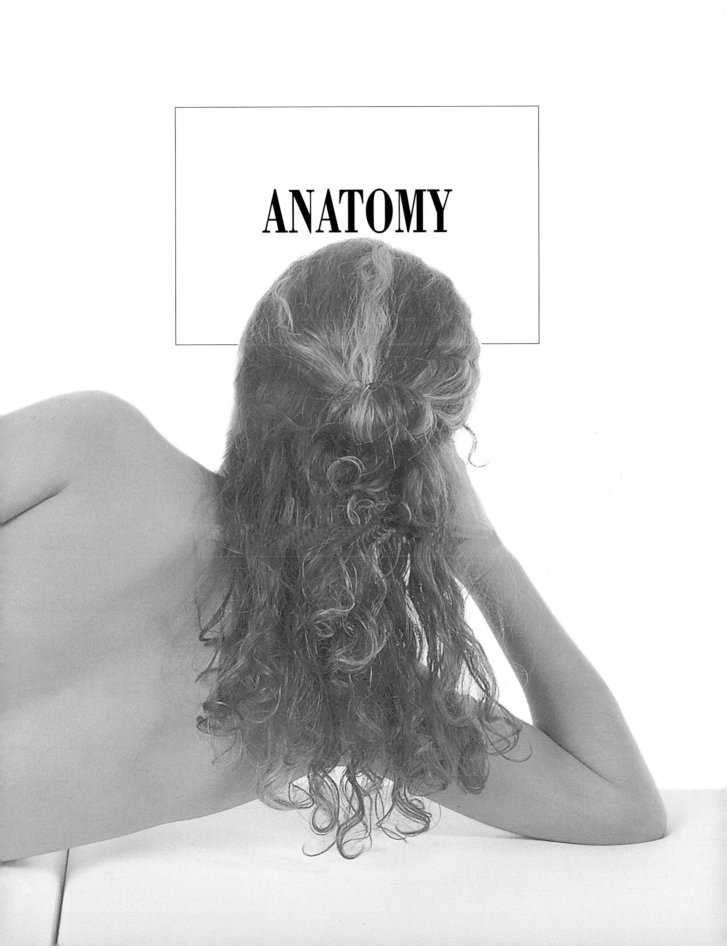

ANATOMY

THE SKIN

When the body is lightly touched, the strongest reactions are felt by the skin. This wonderful, complex structure is able to receive stimuli from without, yet at the same time protects us from a vast number of physical and chemical agents which attack and endanger the equilibrium of the body. Amazingly, on every square centimeter of skin there are on average 3 million cells, 10 hairs, 15 sebaceous glands, 100 sweat glands, 200 pain receiving centers, 25 pressure points for the reception of tactile stimuli, 13 devices for the reception of cold and 2 for heat, 4 meters of nerve fiber, and 3000 cells connected to the sensory organs.

When looked at through a microscope, the skin looks something like the picture depicted on this page. Three layers may be distinguished: the *epidermis*, the external layer; the *dermis*, the intermediate layer; and the *hypodermis*, the subcutaneous adipose tissue.

The epidermis consists of more than one layer of cells which are produced in depth (from the *germinative* layer of the epidermis) and migrate to the surface (the *horny* layer of epidermis) where they then separate. Melanin is found in the germinative layer of the epidermis and determines the color of the skin. The dermis, which is made up of dense *connective tissue* (discussed in depth later), is rich in elastic fibers and has significant vascularization. Numerous *papillae* join the dermis firmly to the epidermis. In the papillae are found

Messner's corpuscles, sense organs which respond to minimal pressure stimuli, and *Krause's receptors*, sense organs of cold. Deeper down in the dermis are *Ruffini's corpuscles,* receptors of heat. Also in the deep areas of the dermis are dispersed about 2 million *sweat glands* which pour out their secretions onto the surface through long excretory ducts. Sweat, evaporating rapidly, cools down the body's surface. Furthermore, the slightly acid secretion of the sweat glands forms a protective shield, preventing bacteria from penetrating into the deepest layers of the skin. *Sebaceous glands*, also lying deep in the dermis, have a reverse function: the layer of wax they produce not only makes the surface of the body soft, but also acts as an insulating material protecting the skin from potential heat loss.

The hypodermis is made up not only of *loose connective tissue*, but also of *adipose tissue* (fat), more or less abundant, which fills in the numerous spaces formed by the connective tissue. Adipose tissue serves as a nutritional deposit and also insulates against too rapid changes in temperature because it is a bad heat conductor. It also protects the structures beneath it, especially in the foot in the form of cushions. In the hypodermis are *Vater-Pacini's corpuscles,* which are also pressure stimuli receptors.

Hairs are horny annexes of the skin. They are elastic and are formed by a cylindrical stem emerging from the epidermis and by deep roots with bulbs in the dermis. Surrounding the hair at the root is the *pilipherous follicle*, a small smooth muscle which causes the hair to stand erect. It lives in the dermis and, through contraction of its fibers, causes horripilation (goosebumps). Furthermore, through its contraction, this muscle exerts a pressure on the sebaceous glands which causes them to empty. During massage, the skin assumes a very important role, for it is through contact with it that the practitioner's hands transmit stimuli into the body. Through the skin, the hands of the expert can "read" and interpret a patient's condition, and that expert may be able to decipher signals coming from internal organs suffering

malfunction, before symptoms of clear organic illness become manifest. During each massage, always observe and analyze your partner's skin condition and aim to refine your hands' perceptive abilities.

THE CONNECTIVE TISSUE

All substances which support the body and link different tissues to each other are called *connective tissues*. Therefore, *bones, cartilages, ligaments and tendons* (*fibrous* connective tissue), *fat and blood vessels* are all considered specialized connective tissues. Common nonspecialized connective tissues also exist within the body. These act as bonding agents, joining and linking together many body structures near each other, yet still allowing a certain degree of movement. This common tissue is called *loose connective tissue*. Loose connective tissue is made up of collagen and elastic fibers immersed in a soft and viscous substance capable of absorbing great quantities of water. As already mentioned, the hypodermis is made up of common loose connective tissue and fat tissue distributed in varying amounts. Nerve fibers that communicate to nerve centers are distributed within the connective tissue. This information allows the nervous system to regulate constantly the functions of the connective tissue, such as the supply of blood, water retention, or sensitivity to pain. Massage, especially connective tissue

massage, acts upon the connective tissue, thus influencing the above-mentioned *reflex regulation* mechanisms, and it is able to affect the equilibrium of blood circulation and subcutaneous liquids. The effects of massage are not limited merely to connective tissue, but extend to the structures beneath the part of the body being massaged. Years of experience and in-depth research in neurophysiology have shown that stimulation in a certain part of the skin always produces a *reflex response* in the analogous internal organs and muscular groups, so much so that maps have been drawn of the skin surface which are used both for diagnosing and for treating illnesses connected with internal organs and muscles.

THE DERMATOMES

The body's surface is divided into parts, or areas, called *dermatomes*, each of which is innervated by a spinal nerve. The same nerve innervates a series of muscles and internal organs. The group of muscles with the same innervation is called a *myotome*, while the group of internal organs with the same innervation is called an *enterotome*. Through the innervation of the same spinal nerve dermatomes, myotomes and enterotomes are closely linked to one another, and any change in one is always reflected in the other two.

At the same time, any kind of massage carried out on the dermatome is transmitted in a reflex way to the corresponding myotomes and enterotomes. However, it is necessary to point out that, topographically-speaking, the dermatome, myotome and enterotome do not always correspond. Intercostal muscles, for example, which are situated roughly near the tenth spinal vertebrae, correspond to a dermatome situated lower down in the lumbar region. It is possible to purchase specific maps that highlight the correspondence between the dermatomes, myotomes, and enterotomes; these are of great help when diagnosing or treating a patient through connective tissue massage.

THE MUSCULAR SYSTEM

The muscular system carries out the functions of movement, thanks to its characteristics of *contractibility, stretchability,* and *elasticity.* Muscles are essential for maintaining posture, and they produce most of the heat necessary to the body. They are divided into three different types. The *cardiac* muscle, the muscle of the heart, is made up of striated fibers. *Smooth* muscles are made up of smooth fibers and are found in the internal organs. They function independently under the control of the vegetative nervous system. *Striated* muscles, made up of striated fibers, are also known as skeletal muscles because they are attached to the bones and allow body movement and walking. They are under voluntary control. Muscles are of different shapes and sizes and are surrounded by a fascia of fibrous connective tissue (*epimysium*); the same connective tissue enfolds fasciae of muscle fibers (*perimysium*) and the single fibers within each sheet of fascia (*endomysium*). Muscles are attached to the bones through fibrous structures known as *tendons* or directly through fleshy fibers (*fleshy insertion*). The fleshy part of the muscle is sometimes interrupted by a connective lamina known as *aponeurosis,* which is attached to the surrounding structures and has a strong and resistant nature. An example of aponeurosis is found in the inner thigh. While functioning, muscles use oxygen carried by the blood to oxidize the substances needed for muscular contraction and subsequent heat production. If the oxygen is not enough to satisfy the complicated chemical processes, then alternative chemical reactions take place and *lactic acid* is produced which causes subsequent muscle weariness. Massage helps the body to reabsorb the lactic acid, which is then synthesized and carried on to the liver.

Each fiber observes the all-or-nothing rule, so contraction either does not take place or takes place to a maximum degree. A greater muscular contraction is obtained from the sum of the contractions of a greater number of fibers of the same muscle. This number of active fibers may change: the skeletal muscles undergo an aging process known as *fibrosis* wherein some of the muscular fibers degenerate and are gradually replaced by nonelastic, noncontractible and nonextendable fibrous connective tissue. Massage helps to delay this irreversible process. There are three main types of muscle contraction.

Tonic contraction: different groups of fibers contract in succession, keeping the muscle in constant tension. As a result, all healthy individuals possess, when awake, constant muscular tone which allows them to maintain posture. Muscle tone above normal is called *spasticity,* while muscle tone below the normal is known as *flaccidity.* We maintain this tone unconsciously and semiautomatically.

Isotonic contraction: (*iso*=same *tono*=tension) is the contraction whereby the tone remains constant within the muscle, and its shortening causes movement. During *isometric* contraction, on the other hand, the length remains unvaried, while the muscle tone increases. This happens, for example, when we push our arms against a wall. The wall obviously does not move, but the effort causes an increase in the muscle tone.

A muscle constantly receiving contraction stimuli contracts with increasing intensity and rapidity until its fibers can no longer relax. At this point there arises what is known as the contraction phenomenon, something which may be significantly reduced by massage.

If a muscle is called on to stretch itself beyond its elastic possibilities, this may result in a minor trauma (*strain*) or a major injury such as a torn ligament (*sprain*) or a complete rupture of the muscular venter. The best way for these ruptures to heal initially is through inactivity, but fibrous scar tissue will form there where the rupture took place. This scar tissue resulting from the healing process may be reduced through massage and exercise.

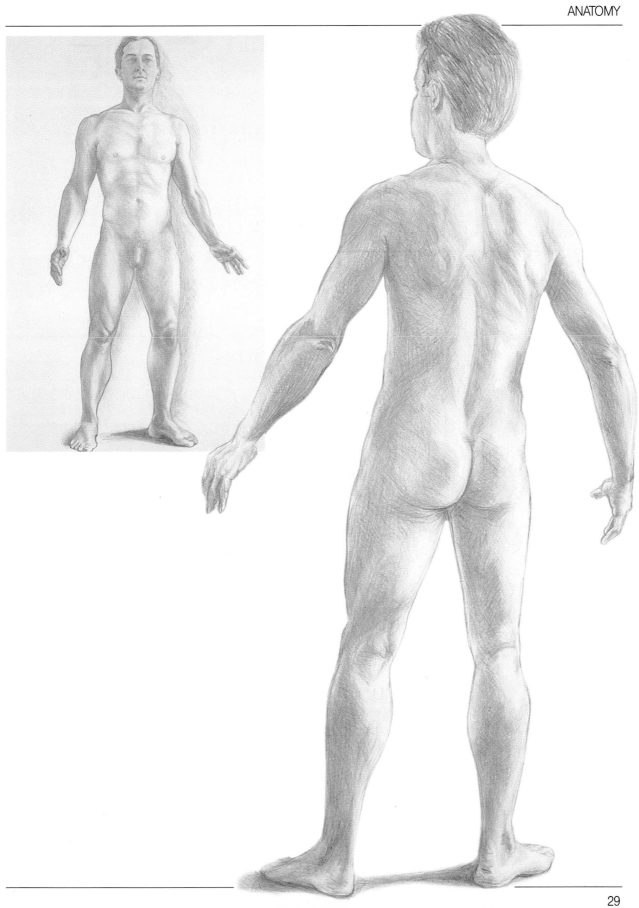

THE CIRCULATORY SYSTEM

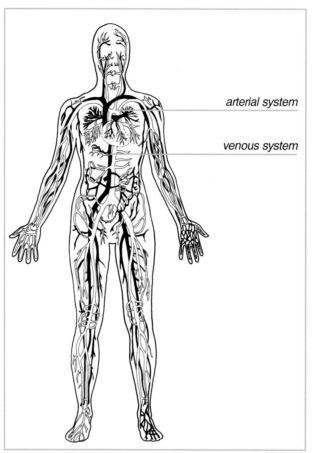

arterial system

venous system

The main function of the circulatory system is to carry essential substances to all the cells of the body and to remove from them the waste products that form during metabolism. The *heart* supplies the necessary energy for the blood to circulate throughout the body, and it does this by automatically contracting (*systole*) and relaxing (*dyastole*) to a rhythm corresponding to the needs of the body. Arteries carry the blood from the heart to the tissues; their walls are resistant, contractible, and elastic and, as they go farther from the heart, they divide into smaller arteries called *arterioles*, into smaller *capillaries*. At this point they form into small veins and then into larger veins. *Veins* carry the blood, full of waste products and carbon dioxide, back to the heart; they are less rich in elastic fibers, but are provided with valves that facilitate the blood's return. Rich in carbon dioxide, venous blood reaches the heart through the superior and inferior vena cava; from here it is sent to the lungs to be reoxygenated and then returns to the heart which pumps it into the aorta in order to disperse it as arterial blood again. Blood distribution to the various organs is regulated by the *autonomic nervous system* which permits a greater supply to those organs or muscles engaged in any form of activity. The systolic pressure of a healthy adult male is about 120/130 millimeters of mercury; diastolic pressure, instead, is around 70/80 millimeters of mercury. In women, values are slightly lower, and lower again in infants. Remember that massage lowers pressure values; therefore a person suffering from low blood pressure should receive a gentle massage in order to avoid possible collapse. The venous return is much more complex than the arterial circulation. This is because veins are devoid of muscular fibers, and they generally must work against gravity. The whole muscular system, with its contraction and relaxation processes, acts as a support pump for venous return. Massage stimulates and strengthens this secondary function of the muscles. At the same time as descreasing blood pressure and improving venous return, massage increases blood volume, boosting arterial circulation. Therefore, a strong, long, and complete massage subjects the heart to greater stress and is therefore not advisable for patients with cardiovascular problems.

The distribution of blood to the different body parts is regulated, according to need, by the *vegetative nervous system* which, through a series of complex biofeedback mechanisms, causes vasodilatation or vasoconstriction reactions in the capillaries, especially in the connective tissue. Through reflex mechanisms, massage significantly influences the capacity for self-regulation of the blood distribution, causing an increase in blood flow in the massaged area (*hyperemia*).

THE LYMPHATIC SYSTEM

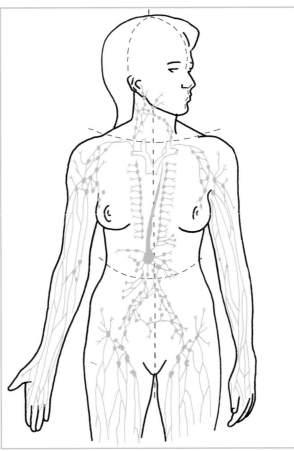

Lymph is a clear and transparent liquid that flows through the interstitial spaces among cells carrying nutritious elements. The lymphatic *plasma* make-up is similar to that of the blood plasma. Lymph is less rich in proteins and carbohydrates, but richer in lipids. The numerous, delicate *lymphatic capillaries* have their source in the blood capillary network and may reach 100 millimicrons. Lymphatic capillaries are made up of more permeable *endothelial cells* than blood capillaries; in their *lumen* (or interior), as with veins, there are valves which direct the flow in a single direction, that is, from the periphery of the body to the central areas. Larger lymphatic veins have more complex walls. In fact, besides the endothelial lining, they have a smooth, muscular lining with long, internal, longitudinal bands, intermediate rings and longitudinal exteriors. All the lymphatic veins flow into two main branches: the *right lymphatic vein* and the *thoracic duct.* These two lymphatic veins flow into the *terminus*, where the *internal jugular* and *subclavicular veins* meet. The lymphatic system differs from the blood system in that it is not a self-contained circuit, but is exclusively a drainage system originating from the peripheral area. In the case of lymph, the propulsion of the circulating fluid is caused by the contraction of the muscles surrounding the lymphatic veins. Another factor is the increase in the intra-abdominal pressure associated with the

decrease in intrathoracic pressure during the inspiration phase of *diaphragmatic breathing.* This means that deep breathing actually helps to facillitate the movement of lymph. As the lymph proceeds, there is also a muscular contraction of the lymphatic vein, although this takes place only in the case of the larger lymphatic veins. Normally, the amount of lymph present in the human body is about five liters. Pathological increases due to alterations in the blood system or due to clots cause *edema.*

In intestinal lymphatic veins, the lymph appears milky after the consumption of fats due to the presence of the numerous drops of fat which it carries along. Substances of all types are absorbed into the various organs from the lymph. Therefore, even harmful substances, such as bacteria and toxins, may be introduced through these channels. *Lymph nodes,* however, form barriers to this process. Oval-shaped formations varying in size from 2 to 20 millimeters, their task is to produce *lymphocytes.* Lymph nodes are particularly numerous in the armpit, in the elbow, around the groin, in the popliteal fossa (the area behind the knee), in the neck, and under the jaw. Also rich in lymph nodes are the *mesentery* (the peritonial fold which supports the small intestine) and the lung *hilum* (the opening through which veins and nerves enter an organ). In fact, every organ of the body is enriched with particular groups of lymph nodes.

SWEDISH MASSAGE

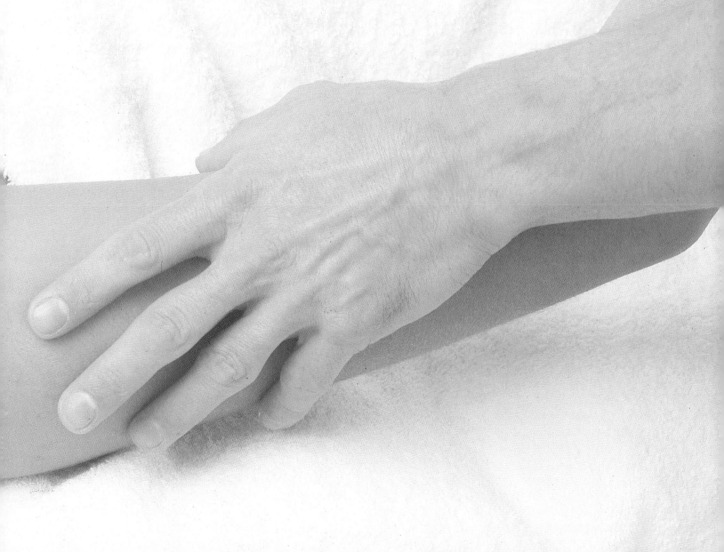

THEORY

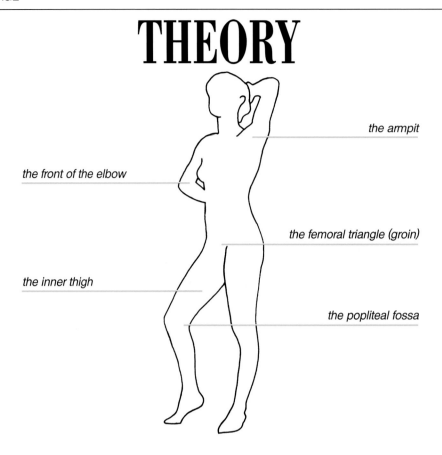

the armpit

the front of the elbow

the femoral triangle (groin)

the inner thigh

the popliteal fossa

MAIN AREAS OF MASSAGE

As we shall see, there are five Swedish massage techniques: *stroking, friction, kneading, percussion, and vibration.* These techniques should follow in sequence and sometimes be taking into account the overall goal and the areas to be worked on. There are three such areas:

- *The superficial level,* consisting of the epidermis and the superficial dermis with their tactile corpuscles, nerve endings, and rich peripheral blood supply. Stroking, both light and sustained, friction, and vibration all access this level.

- *The intermediate level,* which consists of the middle and deep dermis and the subcutaneous cellular tissues. This is the classic connective tissue site, with its cells, in a matrix of elastic and collagen fibers. Massage can greatly affect the density and texture of this area. Friction and kneading access this level.

- *The deepest level,* which consists of the various muscular groups, the nerve plexus, veins, and certain organs with hormonal functions which may be influenced through reflex responses. Strong kneading, consisting of both kneading and squeezing movements, is suitable for this area as are percussion, deep friction and static pressure. The general well-being of your partner, as well as the state of the area involved, should determine the force, depth, and rhythm of these techniques.

PARTS OF THE BODY TO BE AVOIDED

In Swedish massage, there are parts of the body which should not be worked on because they are full of large, superficial nerves. Massaging these areas may cause irritation, sometimes with serious consequences. These areas are:
- the armpit;
- the popliteal fossa (back of the knee);
- the front of the elbow;
- the inner thigh;
- the femoral triangle (the groin).
Furthermore, I would like to remind you that a massage inexpertly carried out may create intolerance, a sense of weariness, nervous excitement, insomnia, or bruises because it is done too deeply, too quickly, or is basically out of accordance with the patient's needs.

THE EFFECTS OF SWEDISH MASSAGE

DIRECT OR MECHANICAL MASSAGE AND ITS EFFECTS ON MUSCLES

- It facilitates the circulation of the blood and of the lymph in the massaged areas of the body.
- It facilitates the shedding of old cells.
- It helps eliminate the sebaceous exudates, thus making the skin softer and more elastic.
- It accelerates the turnover of the treated tissues.
- By stimulating the circulation, it assists the greater supply of nutritive substances to the areas massaged and a more rapid elimination of metabolic waste.
- It helps dissolve organic deposits and restore elasticity to those muscles which have remained inactive due to immobility. This lack of elasticity is due to an increase in the viscosity of the interstitial liquid.
- It improves the elasticity and the contractile capacity of the treated muscle.
- It helps to reduce muscular and ligamentous tension as well as muscular contractions.
- It helps the joints move with greater ease by removing peri- and endoarticular adhesions, thus facilitating the sliding of articular surfaces.
- It activates and therefore produces tissue plane movement, particularly in the presence of scar tissue or following immobilization.
- It has an analgesic effect on sensitive peripheral nerve terminations and a relaxing effect on motor nerves.
- It positively influences the function of the big veins. If a motor nerve is compressed too hard it loses its excitability; if massaged gently, its sensibility and its powers of conduction increase.

INDIRECT OR REFLEX ACTION AND ITS EFFECTS

- Local stimulation of the vasomotor nerves causes an active hyperemia which manifests itself through heat and a flushness.
- The local temperature is made to rise 2-3 °C.
- The heartbeat becomes calmer and more regular.
- Breathing becomes easier.
- The kidney eliminates liquids and nitrogen solutions.
- Edema and vein stasis due to immobility is reduced.
- And, last but not least, massage brings about psychophysical relaxation.

STROKING

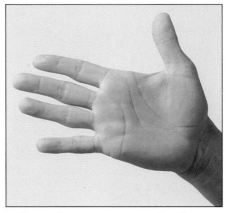

Stroking (also called Effleurage) is simple and intuitive, and is something we all do on instinct when a part of our bodies has been traumatized.
A mother strokes her child while she is bathing it; all beings stroke one another gently to cause pleasant sensations.
The main purpose of stroking, therefore, is to create a general sense of well-being.

THE EFFECTS OF STROKING ON THE SKIN

Stroking helps shed old cells, accelerates the cell substitution process, and eliminates wax, thus making the skin softer and more elastic.
Cutaneous microcirculation may be stimulated both in a mechanical way, that is, by stroking the skin and pinching the capillaries, or by reflex, that is by activating the *vegetative* nervous system.
Vasoconstriction occurs if the stroking technique is carried out gently, whereas vasodilatation takes place if stroking is too strong. In each case, the *tissue renewal* process is set in motion in the areas massaged.

TECHNIQUE

Stroking is carried out with open, relaxed hands gently resting on the part of the person's body needing to be worked upon. Hand and body contact must be total: the whole hand must be touching your partner's body constantly, adapting to its every shape. Pressure must always be minimal and hand contact on the epidermis light. The rhythm is slow and constant; the movements are wide, circular, and enfolding.

In order to increase the relaxing effect, use rose and orange oils.

1 *Coat your hands lightly with oil and place them on the low back.*

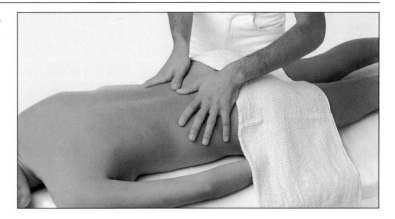

Work toward the head by massaging the muscle fasciae along the spinal column.

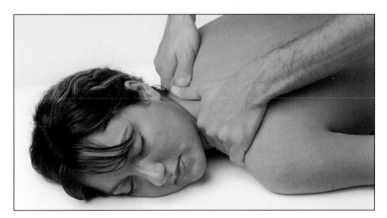

Gently stroke the neck and enfold it sideways, passing beneath the jaw. Slip your hands downwards, along the side of the neck, enfold the shoulder muscles and work over the shoulder blades.

Work down the sides as far as the low back area and bring your hands together to the center on the sacrum (pelvic bone). Repeat this movement several times, trying to keep a steady rhythm.

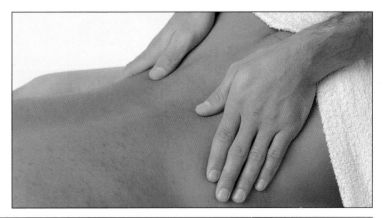

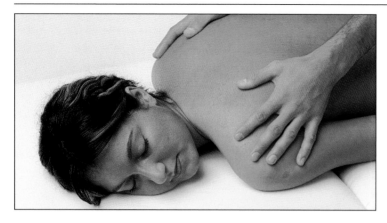

2 *Repeat the previous exercise, this time making even wider movements, embracing part of the arms and the whole lateral side of the chest.*

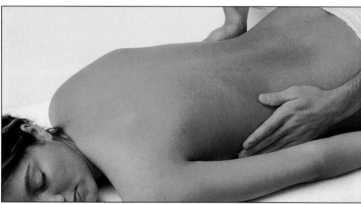

The movement becomes more enveloping, and takes in the sides of the rib cage, the waist, and the hips. Once you have reached the buttocks, work your way back to the center with a circular movement and repeat. Carry out this movement several times, keeping a steady rhythm.

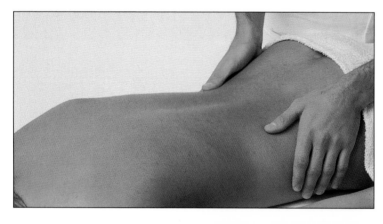

3 *Starting from the sacrum, carry out small circular movements that go from the center to the sides. Slowly work your way toward the shoulders.*

Envelop the shoulders and the arms as far as the elbows. With circular and encircling movements, work toward the shoulders and then down again, along the sides, back to your starting point. Repeat several times.

4 *All these techniques are carried out with synchronous movements of the arms. Try to vary the massage by moving your hands alternately: that is, while your right hand is working up the back, the left hand is working its way down, and the other way round. Repeat the movements described in steps 1-3. From now on the techniques will become more complex. In order to coordinate the movement of your hands, it is essential that you practice constantly. Remember to carry out wide, circular movements keeping a steady rhythm and to touch the side parts of the back.*

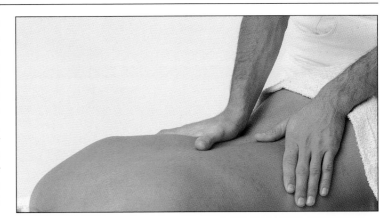

Many of you will probably find that you are unable to coordinate the movements of your hands. The hand you don't usually use (the left one for a right-handed person) may seem to be semiparalyzed and unable to obey your orders. Do not be discouraged, but practice frequently. You will soon notice a significant improvement.

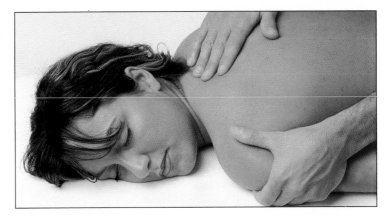

5 *With your right hand draw a huge "eight" on your partner's back. Repeat several times. Then repeat again, this time using your left hand.*

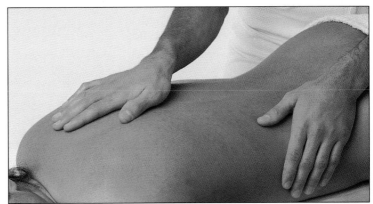

Now try carrying out this exercise with both your hands, your left hand following your right hand at a short distance. Do you find it difficult? Do your arms tend to cross? This is natural at the beginning, but as you get more practice, your partner will begin to feel that exquisite sensation as if he were being massaged by several people at the same time.

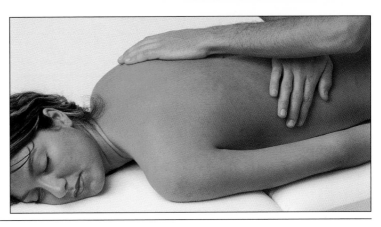

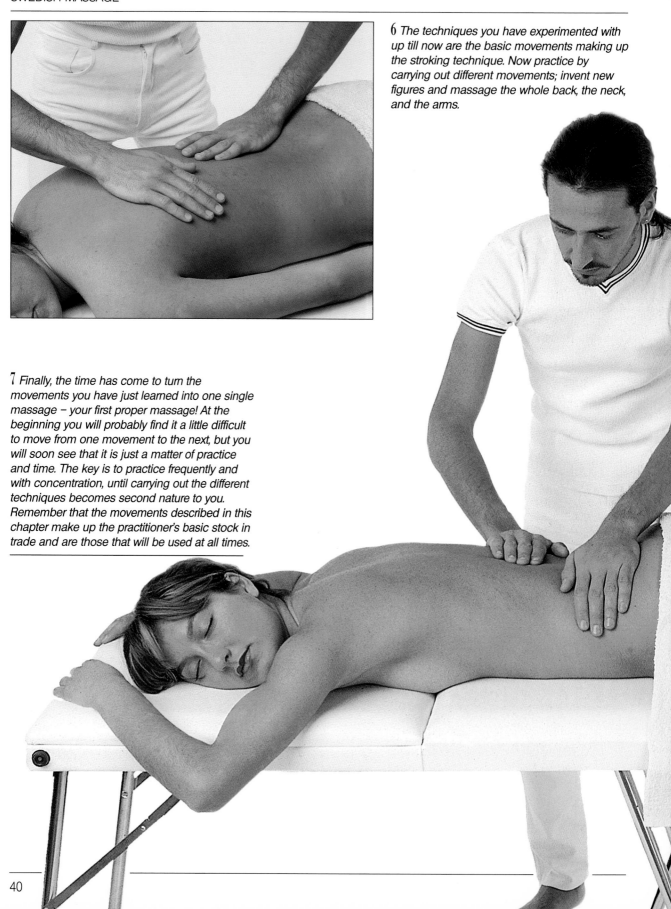

6 The techniques you have experimented with up till now are the basic movements making up the stroking technique. Now practice by carrying out different movements; invent new figures and massage the whole back, the neck, and the arms.

7 Finally, the time has come to turn the movements you have just learned into one single massage – your first proper massage! At the beginning you will probably find it a little difficult to move from one movement to the next, but you will soon see that it is just a matter of practice and time. The key is to practice frequently and with concentration, until carrying out the different techniques becomes second nature to you. Remember that the movements described in this chapter make up the practitioner's basic stock in trade and are those that will be used at all times.

SOME DON'TS

Avoid pressing too hard. The rhythm should not be broken by abrupt variations but should be kept smooth. Never lift your fingertips from your partner's body and always adapt your hands to its shape. Keep your body flexible as if dancing while massaging. Vary the movements to avoid getting bored and to make the massage more interesting. Carry out circular movements, avoiding any sudden changes in direction.

WHEN ADVISABLE

As we have seen, stroking, because of its particular features, is advisable in all those cases where the other techniques do not work or may be harmful. Light stroking may be practiced on people who are weak or ill; on children and on the elderly; on pregnant women and on excitable and highly-strung people. Stroking is to be recommended for calming states of anxiety and inducing deep relaxation. It is an extremely efficient beauty treatment for the skin.

WHEN NOT ADVISABLE

Patients with infectious diseases and contagious skin diseases which could be transmitted through bodily contact should not be treated.

TO CONCLUDE

Stroking is massage par excellence. It is simple, efficient, and normally has no negative side effects. It is the cornerstone of Swedish massage and it begins and ends all treatments. Always do some stroking between different techniques, particularly when these are carried out with particular intensity.

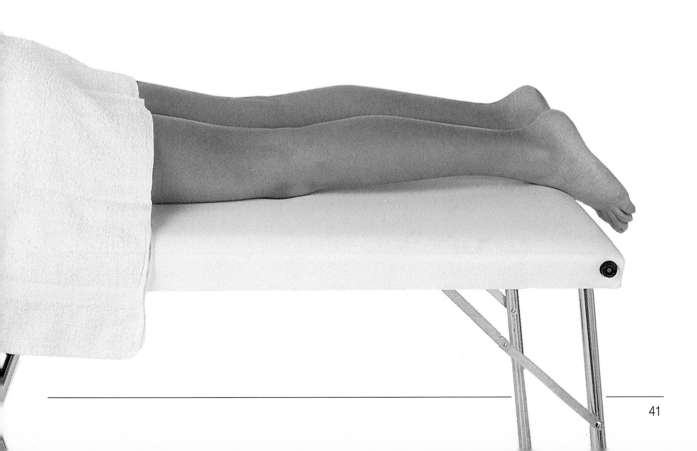

FRICTION

The vasodilatory effect of friction can be heightened by using essence of camphor and thyme.

Technically speaking, friction is similar to stroking, but it differs significantly in its intensity and in the effects it produces.

THE EFFECTS OF FRICTION ON THE CONNECTIVE TISSUE AND THE SKIN

Friction produces an intense *local skin vasodilation* and directly causes the tissues to drain, disposing of waste products and letting good nutrients in. It affects the connective tissue positively, activating them and reducing adhesions caused by prolonged inactivity or following surgery. Friction acts directly on the skin because of the contact between the practioner's hands and the patient's skin. As a consequence, heat is developed and blood flows to the surface of the treated area. By reflex, a series of reactions is triggered in the vegetative nervous system which causes the

muscles and the organs linked to the dermatome to relax.

TECHNIQUE

Friction is carried out on the larger surfaces (the back, for example) with the palm of the hand and particularly with the *tenar* and *hypotenar* eminences (the most fleshy parts of the palm). On smaller surfaces, the fingertips or the side of the hand are used. Pressure is significantly stronger than with stroking. This is because the deepest levels, such as the connective levels are to be stimulated without involving the muscular tissue. The rhythm is slower and the direction is centripetal, semicircular, or transversal. In some cases (such as, before a sports competition) friction must be fast and sustained. In this way, the local temperature is increased and circulation stimulated, with positive effects on muscle oxygenation.

1 *Repeat the movements given for stroking, increasing, however, the pressure and slowing down the rhythm. In the return phase, when your hands move from the shoulders toward the lumbar region, pressure will be similar to that of stroking.*

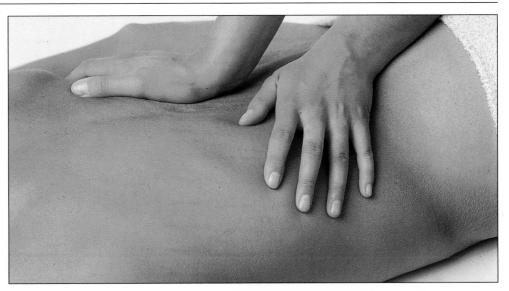

2 *Rub the cervical region (neck) with both thumbs, while the palm of each hand, resting on the corresponding shoulder, grips the trapezium muscle. The thumbs rotate together or alternatively around the seventh cervical vertebrae (the most protruding one at the base of the neck) and move toward the neck and the shoulders with circular motions.*

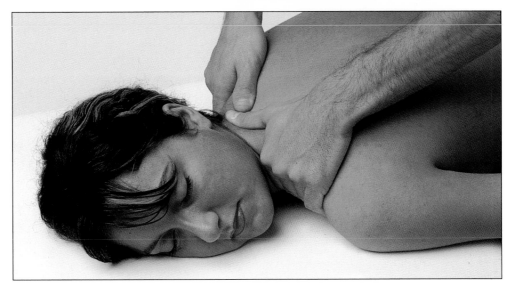

3 *Repeat the previous exercise on the sacrum. Here use thumb pressure, deciding how much is appropriate without causing discomfort, and produce local hyperemia (temporary redness indicating increased circulation). Your alternate circular motions should widen in diameter until they cover the entire region.*

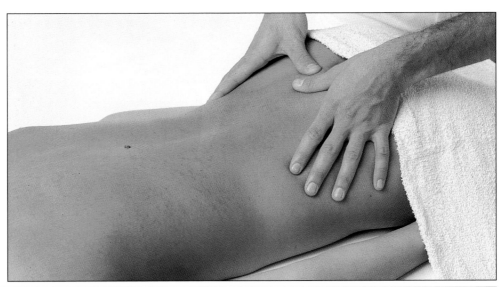

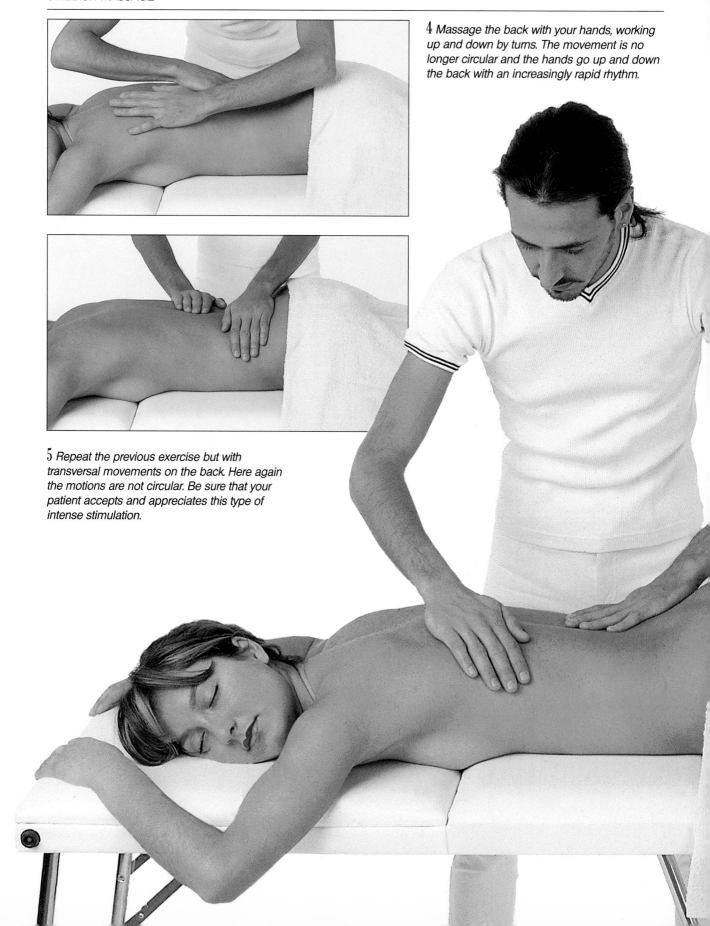

4 *Massage the back with your hands, working up and down by turns. The movement is no longer circular and the hands go up and down the back with an increasingly rapid rhythm.*

5 *Repeat the previous exercise but with transversal movements on the back. Here again the motions are not circular. Be sure that your patient accepts and appreciates this type of intense stimulation.*

SOME DON'TS

Do not press too hard. Remember that in the return phase, pressure must not be exerted too hard. Never rub in a centrifugal direction (from the shoulders toward the feet). Avoid friction on painful or particularly sensitive areas.

WHEN ADVISABLE

Friction is recommended in cases of adhesion of the connective tissues following prolonged inactivity or after surgery, particularly when orthopedic. It is carried out with the fingertips and helps to reabsorb infiltrates, hematoma, and exudates. It causes a strong local hyperemia, helpful in degenerative diseases such as arthrosis.

WHEN NOT ADVISABLE

It is absolutely not advisable to rub an inflamed or infected region caused by phlebitis or capillary fragility. Severe varicose veins are in this latter category. Do not massage after a recent trauma, but allow healing powers to follow their natural course.

TO CONCLUDE

Friction is an intense and efficient technique, but must be carried out carefully. Practice at length, and study the effects it has on the body. Friction is the first technique you've learned here that produces noticeable physiological reactions in the body.

6 Carry out friction with alternate circular movements so fast as to produce skin hyperemia.

KNEADING

Kneading is the most complex technique in Swedish massage and acts upon the muscular masses, the deepest dermis, and the connective tissue.

THE EFFECTS OF KNEADING ON MUSCLES AND THE CONNECTIVE TISSUE

Light kneading promotes *drainage* of the interstitial liquid and empties the glands found in the skin. It acts on the connective tissue causing *adhesions* to break apart and the squeezing action on the muscles helps in the *liquid renewal process*, thereby increasing *elasticity* and *tone*. A further benefit is represented by improved circulation and *deep vasodilatation*.

TECHNIQUE

Kneading is mainly carried out with the thumb in opposition to the index finger. With the "pliers" thus formed, grasp the muscle and with both hands squeeze alternately, moving along the longitudinal axis of the muscle in a centripetal direction. If the muscular mass is large, the "pliers" are formed by all the fingers opposing the thumb and the tenar eminence. The movement is similar to that of kneading bread and the rhythm must be steady. There are several kneading variations, each used to obtain specific results:
- *fluffing* is carried out by grasping the cutaneous fold and letting it fall again. This causes the separation of the subcutaneous connective tissue from the underlying tissues.
- *fanning* is carried out with both thumbs held near each other and pushing the skin in a centripetal direction, raising it while the other fingers carry on "walking" on the skin and helping to raise it in the direction of the thumbs. Fanning causes the separation of the connective tissue on wide surfaces and, at the same time, brings about a positive vegetative reaction (relaxation) with hyperemia and vasodilation.

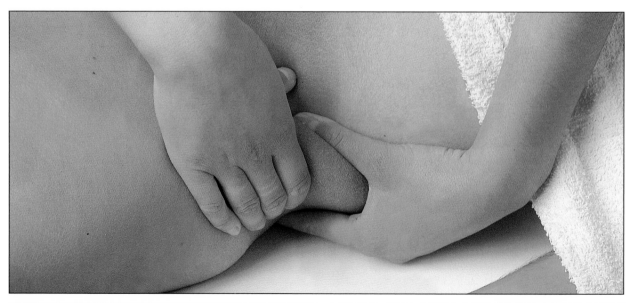

1 *With circular movements of the fingertips, knead all the paravertebral muscles, both left and right. These are the long muscles adjacent to the spine on either side that stretch from the head to the sacrum. Begin in the lumbar region and work toward the shoulders and back. Repeat several times.*

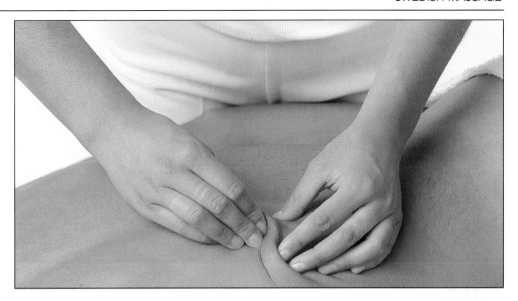

2 *Knead the larger muscles, such as those of the back. Begin from your partner's side, grasping the muscle with both hands and alternating them with lifting squeezing movements, while working upwards as far as the armpits. Return where you began with a long stroking movement. Repeat several times on both sides of the body.*

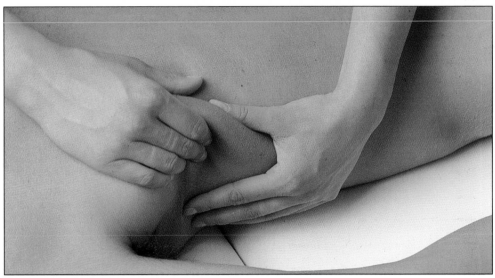

3 *Knead the muscles of the shoulders and of the neck, using the fingertips of the index and middle fingers in opposition to the thumbs, but exerting less pressure than in the previous exercise.*

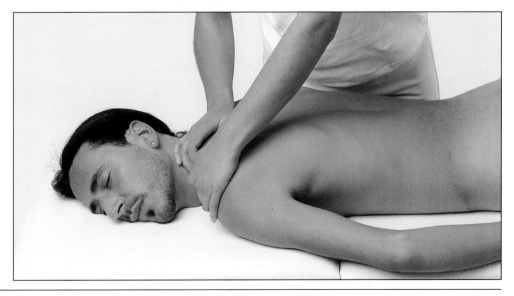

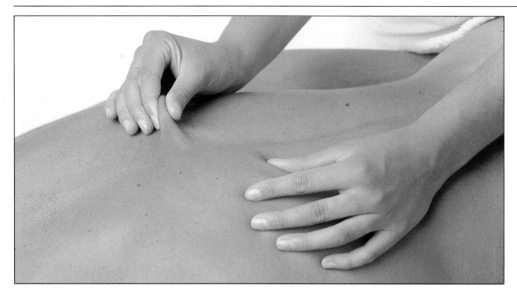

4 *Return to the paravertebral muscles and knead the tissues by grasping the skin folds with both thumbs and the index fingers. Alternating your hands, work as far as the shoulders and down again with stroking movements. Repeat several times, trying to keep a steady rhythm.*

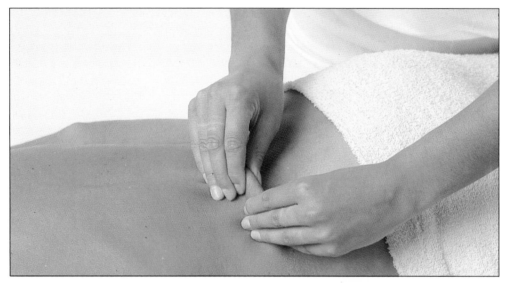

5 *Still working on the paravertebral muscles, raise the skin fold by pushing with your thumbs beginning from the lumbar region. Work as far as the shoulders, imparting the direction of the movement with the other fingers. Return to the lumbar region with a stroking movement and repeat several times, keeping in mind the indications set out above.*

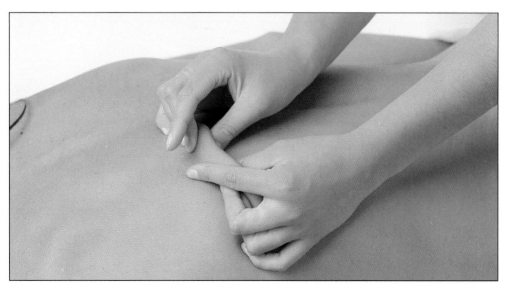

Knead the entire back several times using all of the variations described.

SOME DON'TS

Avoid causing pain. Should this happen inadverently, it means that the pressure was too deep, was applied too quickly, or was incorrectly placed. Never knead in a centrifugal direction, for example, from the shoulders toward the lumbar region. Do not insist on kneading a muscle which is too tense, but carry out lighter movements; only when you feel it is more relaxed, should you try to knead it again. Kneading which is carried out in an incorrect manner almost always manifests itself with bruises which give witness to the practitioner's incompetence. Always alternate kneading with other, lighter techniques.

WHEN ADVISABLE

Kneading has positive effects on infiltrates, and softens and relaxes tired muscles. It restores elasticity and resistance by stimulating vital energy and activating cellular renewal processes. Kneading can free chemical substances such as acetylcholine, which influences the metabolism of the skin's sugar reserves. Consequently, it provides the underlying muscles with glycogen, which is essential for performing physical labor. It is advisable in cases of edema and cellulitis, and for softening tissues which have become stiffened by prolonged inactivity, muscular fatigue, atrophy and rheumatism.

WHEN NOT ADVISABLE

Do not knead inflamed tissues or those healing after a trauma. Do not use this technique in the presence of phlebitis, varicose veins, or fragile capillary veins.

TO CONCLUDE

Kneading is essential for treating muscular problems. With this technique, you begin to show your natural ability and aptitude for this art. Remember, however, that constant practice can bring your hidden talents to the surface, and do not despair if at the beginning you face seemingly insurmountable difficulties.

VIBRATION

Vibration is a movement carried out on the skin, which is transmitted from one part of the underlying muscular, fleshy body to the other. It is a tiring technique and a difficult one to put into practice.

THE EFFECTS OF VIBRATION ON NERVE ENDINGS

Vibration works on the cutaneous, subcutaneous, and muscular nerve terminations. It has a *sedative* effect, but also acts upon the main substance of the connective tissue making it more *malleable* when *flocculation* or *clotting* (adhesions, healing processes, scars) occurs.

TECHNIQUE

Vibration is produced with the practitioner's hand stretched out flat on the surface needing treatment. This hand exerts measured, intermittent, quivering pressures. It is similar to a wave which is transmitted in depth, and it affects the nerve endings. It may also be performed with the fingertips. Frequency and intensity may be varied in different ways.

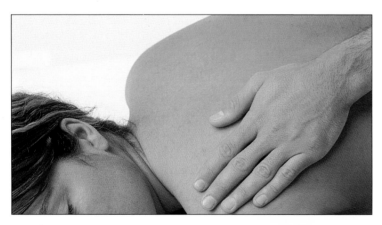

1 *Place the palm of your hand on the dorsal region, above the shoulder blade, and carry out short, rhythmical movements to the right and left. The skin must flow above the subcutaneous tissues. Repeat the same movement above the other scapula.*

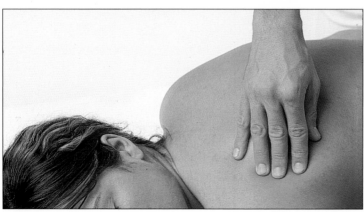

2 *Repeat the previous exercise, this time using your fingertips. Try to keep a steady rhythm and try to vary the pressure so that the vibration will reach depths.*

3 *Repeat the two previous exercises on the sacral region, on the buttocks, on the thighs, and on the lumbar region. This technique, as you will notice, is tiring to the practitioner, and may not be done for more than 30 seconds.*

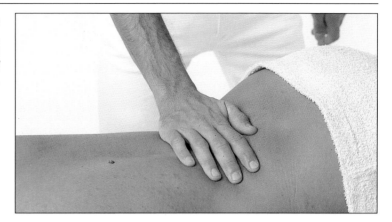

4 *Still using one hand, repeat exercises from 1 to 3, this time, however, without keeping a rhythmical movement but carrying out a very light vibration which starts from the center of your abdomen and which, through your arm, transmits deep into your partner's body. In the first phase of the technique (exercises 1, 2, and 3), the effect is similar to that produced by a vibromasseur, while in this second phase (exercise 4), the effect is similar to the vibrations caused by an ultrasound machine.*

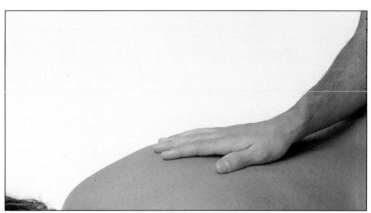

SOME DON'TS

Avoid sliding the palm of your hand on the skin, ensuring that the cleavage (a surface on which the sliding produced by the massage is transmitted) is represented by the connective tissue and other subcutaneous tissues. Always keep a steady rhythm and do not press too hard on the soft regions of the skin which cover delicate internal organs, for example, in areas such as the abdomen or belly.

WHEN ADVISABLE

Vibration has both a sedative and a relaxing effect. If it is very light and contained (as in exercise 4), it calms the overexcitability of the motor and sensory nerves. If applied to the muscles of the face, vibration can help to smooth out wrinkles. According to some authors, vibration can be helpful for chill blains or asthma (carrying out vibration on the third and fourth cervical vertebra), and is effective if done for rehabilitation purposes after a paralysis of the facial nerve.

WHEN NOT ADVISABLE

Do not carry out vibration on an inflamed region or on the most delicate parts of the body. If the skin or the subcutaneous connective tissue is either irritated or hypersensistive, vibration may bring about painful responses and is in any case very badly tolerated.

TO CONCLUDE

Vibration is a delicate and difficult technique to perform. Carry it out on young, strong patients and only if you want to obtain a sedative effect: athletes who suffer from muscle pain and muscle spasms are those who benefit most from this technique.

PERCUSSION

Although an interesting to watch and well-known technique, percussion is not a particularly effective one. It is carried out with the flat or the edge of the hand or with the hand cupped. The technique must be gentle and needs to be well-tolerated in order to be helpful.

THE EFFECTS OF PERCUSSION

Percussion causes strong hyperemia and therefore improves local nutrition. It stimulates the *elasticity* of the muscular fibers and, if repeated for a sufficient amount of time, diminishes *nervous excitability*. Slapping and cupping are techniques used almost exclusively for aesthetic massage, to produce a greater blood flow in the gluteal and hip regions when these have a lot of adipose tissue. As seen in the sections on anatomy, this is a sign of very low blood supply. This technique, carried out with the side of the hand and with relaxed fingers, especially if performed gently, is often used in the final phase of a therapeutic massage for muscle spasms and pains.

TECHNIQUE

Percussion is made up of different techniques:
- *Slapping* is carried out with hands flat and gently "slapping" the region that needs treatment.
- *Cupping* is carried out with cupped hands, which on striking on the cutaneous surface, trap a volume of air which instantly compresses the underlying tissues.
The correct performance of this technique generates a characteristic "popping" noise.
- *Tapotement* is carried out with open hands, the fingers being spread wide and relaxed.
It is the *ulnar* on the little finger side which strikes the skin rhythmically.
The relaxed fingers produce a string of repercussions as they rapidly strike one another from the little to the index finger.
- There is a stronger form of the hand technique which uses the hand's *ulnar edge* (from the little finger to the wrist), but as this is excessively sharp, it is not advised.

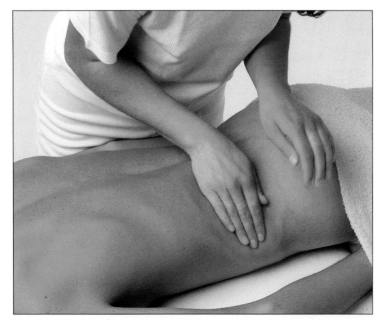

1 *With both your hands, slap your partner's buttocks and sides repeatedly and rhythmically.*

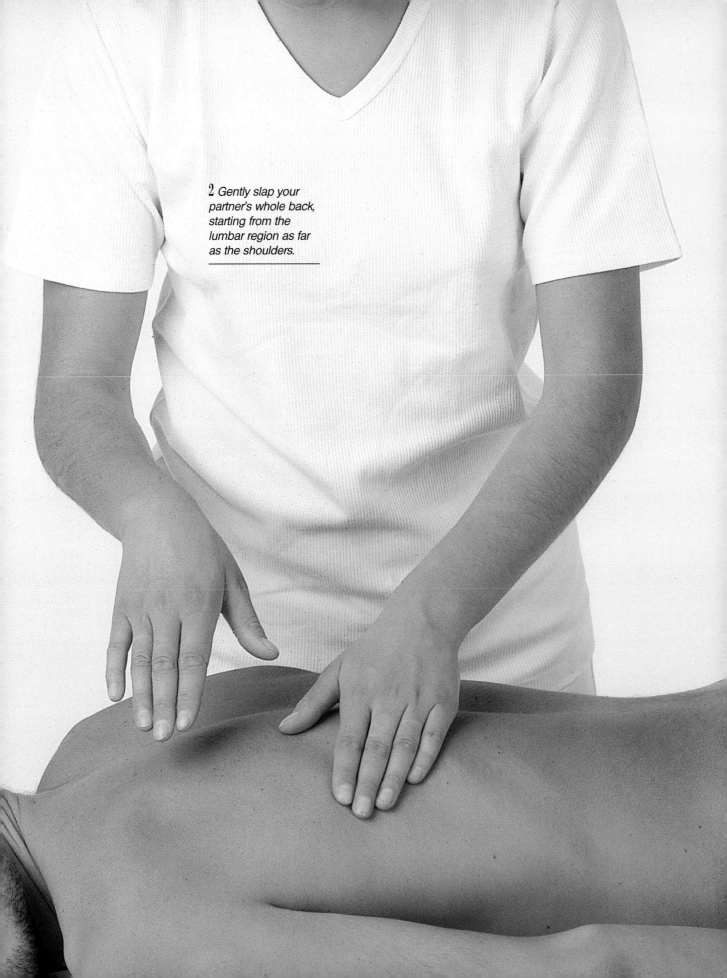

2 *Gently slap your partner's whole back, starting from the lumbar region as far as the shoulders.*

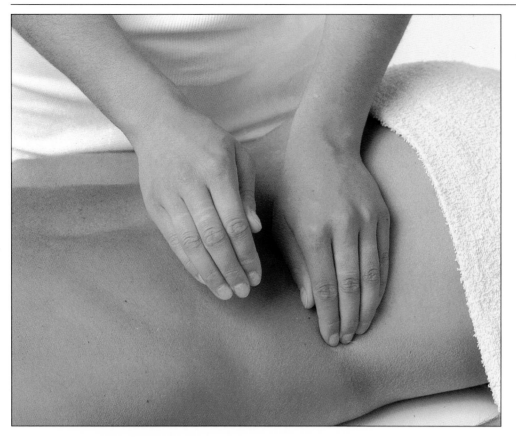

3 *Cup the buttocks and sides with both your hands. Listen to how different the noise of cupping is compared to that of slapping.*

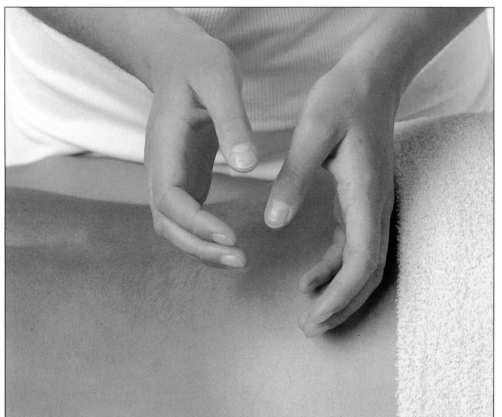

4 *Carry out tapotement on the buttocks with both your hands, trying to keep a steady rhythm. Keep your fingers relaxed and carry out wrist movements.*

5 *Continue the percussion technique, moving from the lumbar region as far as the shoulders, following the paravertebral muscles. Repeat several times, until you reach the necessary coordination, and maintain a steady rhythm.*

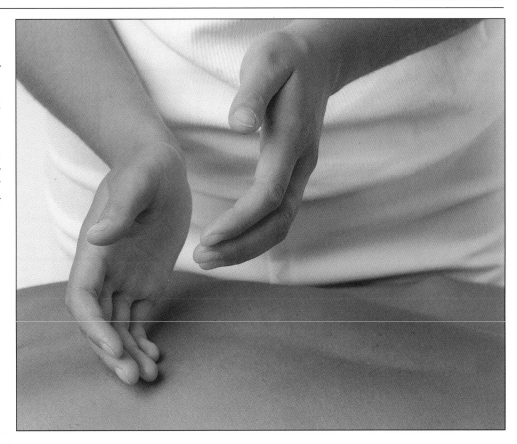

SOME DON'TS

Avoid carrying out movements too energetically. You must never provoke pain or sense of fastidiousness. Try to keep a steady rhythm.

WHEN ADVISABLE

Cupping and slapping are generally used in aesthetic treatments in order to stimulate hyperemia and local circulation. Percussion performed with the edge of the hands stimulates elasticity in the muscles. If repeated over a period of time, it has a relaxing effect.

WHEN NOT ADVISABLE

Percussion is not advised in inflammatory conditions, as well as in varicose veins, thrombophlebitis and in patients afflicted with osteoporosis (reduction of calcium in the bones). Obviously, you must not perform the percussion technique on wounds, bruises, or on any areas which have received traumas.

TO CONCLUDE

There is a tendency to abuse this technique because it is enjoyable and seems to have a profound effect. Perform it with caution and only when it is strictly necessary. Be careful not to exceed that which your partner is comfortable with as this can damage the tissues and the organs.

SWEDISH MASSAGE TECHNIQUES BACK MASSAGE

The back is the part of the body which most often enjoys the beneficial effects of massage. Massage in this area is advisable where there is cervical *arthrosis*, *stiff neck*, *spasms*, *pain* deriving from stress, or the aftereffects of traumatic events such as lesions or trauma to the soft tissues of the neck following car accidents (whiplash). Equally important are all those painful manifestations difficult to interpret, which are often accompanied by widespread contractures and joint stiffness.

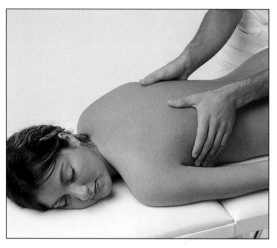

Back massage is not recommended in the presence of joint inflammation (*arthrosis*), inflammation of the peripheral nerves (*neuritis*), osteoporosis, bone cancer, all infectious or inflammatory diseases, or where there are skin diseases which carry the risk of contagion through contact.

All massage techniques are allowed and advised for the back. The movements should be made with the palm of the hand, using wide circular motions on the large muscles (dorsal, lumbar, and trapezius). Around the vertebral joints, the shoulders, and on the neck, you should use the fingertips and the pinch formed by the tenar and hypotenar eminences and the fingers.

The massage should begin with slow, gentle stroking, employing wide circular movements in order to overcome your partner's natural defense reaction. Pressure is then increased to friction with slow, rhythmic movements which will produce superficial hyperemia.

The other Swedish massage techniques follow and complete the treatment, alternating and blending with each other in a continuous, steady rhythm. *Stroking* and *friction* constitute the basic elements of massage and act as a lead-in to the other techniques. Avoid jarring movements and sudden changes in rhythm and keep in constant contact with your partner's skin. Back massage is also excellent for *physical fatigue*, *depression,* and *stress*. In this regard, it is helpful to let your partner talk openly, should that person wish, as this can be freeing from psychological burdens. In this way, massage really becomes a compound therapy which can release latent psychosomatic energies. Sometimes this is expressed in dramatic ways, such as bursts of tears, explosions of laughter, or intense general shaking.

Your task, however, is to guide every phase of the session, avoiding emotional *involvement* in your partner's problems while still remaining empathetic. The qualities required for this attitude are partly innate, but they improve and become more refined during years of contact with different personalities.

Always end back massage with light, diminishing movements, stroking slowly and delicately and, where possible, let your partner rest as long as necessary.

When massaging the shoulders and neck, it is advisable for your partner to sit on a backless chair, with his arms and head leaning on a table. In this position the whole upper back area can be properly treated.

It is also suitable for patients with a stiff neck, those suffering from cervical arthrosis, and for the specific treatment of headaches caused by arthrosis. When you treat, make sure your partner is comfortable and that the legs remain crossed.

LEG MASSAGE

Massage of the legs can be helpful in two ways: it reduces overall tension in the lower body, producing an overall relaxation effect, and it is also of an *aesthetic nature* and is used to eliminate the signs of cellulite and to help mobilize areas where venous stasis exists, reducing swelling and edema in the lower limbs. In these cases, more specific techniques such as *manual lymphatic drainage* or *connective tissue massage* are often added to the Swedish massage. We shall study these techniques in greater depth later. Leg massage is particularly important for athletes and is recommended in the *aftermath of traumatic events* such as fractures, muscle strains, or ligament tears to the knee and/or the ankle. These pathologies force the patient into inactivity which can last for months, causing the muscles to shrink and lose tone, and causing the joints to become stiff. Leg massage should not be performed when there is

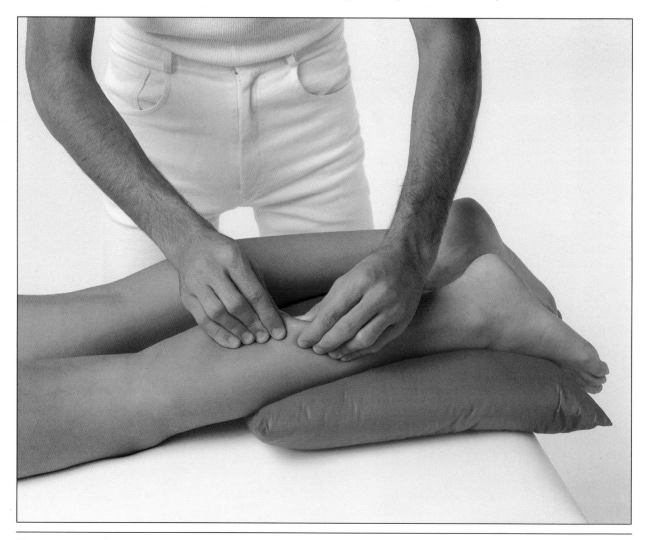

acute inflammation, immediately after a trauma and in cases of thrombophlebitis, varicose veins, or fragile capillaries. The techniques are similar to the ones used for the back, except that the positions of the hands must be adapted to these shapes, which have smaller and more rounded surfaces. Therefore the fingertips and the arch formed by the space between the thumb and the index finger must be used more frequently. Massage behind the

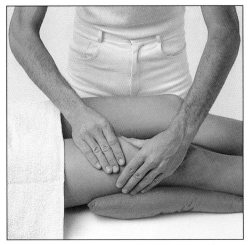

knee, on the inner thigh and on the groin is to be avoided. When massaging the back of the legs, place a rigid cushion under the ankles and while massaging the front put the cushion under the knees. Very often, and particularly during aesthetic massage,

the patient is placed on his side, so as to treat the whole lateral part of the thigh and the flank more satisfactorily. In this case, a fairly large cushion, placed under the folded upper leg, may help. Leg massage is almost always preceded by that of the foot (which is the real peripheral pump and therefore very important for circulation). At this point of your study, perform Swedish massage in this region also, using almost exclusively your fingertips. Later, we will study the specific technique of foot reflexology more in detail. Continue to practice all the exercises relative to leg massage, adapting them to the special shapes of the lower limbs, until you have gained greater confidence.

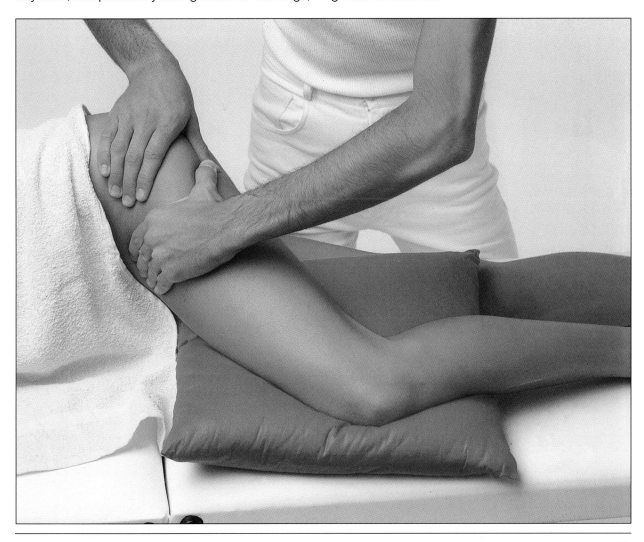

ARM MASSAGE

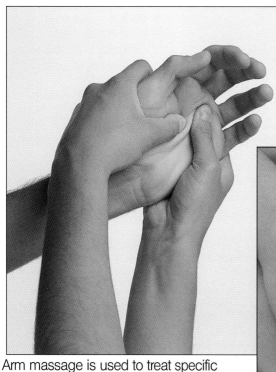

Arm massage is used to treat specific problems such as *arthrosis, tennis elbow, writer's cramp, and rheumatism.*
This massage is also recommended to complete the treatment for cervical arthrosis when this causes congestion of the *brachial plexus*, with painful reactions in arms and hands. This can sometimes manifest itself as *carpal tunnel syndrome.*
Apart from those cases generally not advisable, remember that the arm is never treated during the acute, inflammatory phase of a frozen shoulder, nor immediately after any traumatic event. When massaging the arm, avoid the armpits and the bend of the elbow. This technique is similar to that used for the legs, the only difference being that the surface is smaller, and therefore the movements should be more refined and selective. Practice

frequently on the arms as already suggested on the legs. During arm massage, it does not matter whether your partner is lying supine or prone, or is seated. Try out all these variations several times until you have mastered the techniques in the different positions. Remember always to massage the hand deeply during the arm massage. The hand, in fact, is the seat of important reflex points, and we shall study these in more detail later on in this manual.

FACE MASSAGE

Facial massage is a powerful type of treatment; not only can it smooth out wrinkles and cleanse the face, but also it helps to calm headaches and to balance energy excesses in the top part of the body (in this case massaging the scalp is very effective). The face and the neck are the "opening regions" for *lymphatic drainage* and need a particular technique which we shall study later in this handbook.

In theory, apart from the eyes, there are no areas that should not be massaged because energetic movements are replaced by very gentle movements of the fingertips: very light stroking, drainage from the center toward the temples and the neck, and light kneading of the few fleshy areas.

Do not massage using large quantities of cream; where possible, let your partner choose the cream from among those not causing allergic reactions. While carrying out a facial massage, avoid direct light on your partner's face, and have a background of suitable music to induce maximum muscular relaxation.

Carry out the massage with your partner lying on the floor, a treatment table, or sitting on a comfortable armchair. At the end of the massage, gently rest your hands on your partner's face and hold them there covering the eyes for a minute or so without exerting pressure.

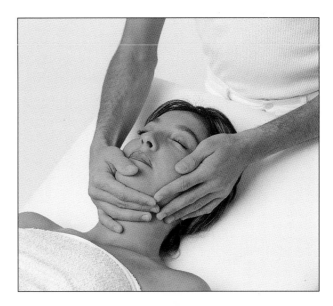

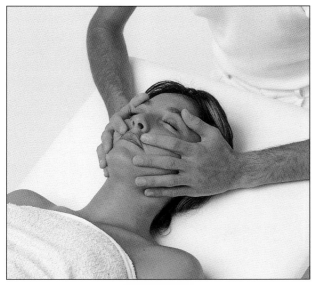

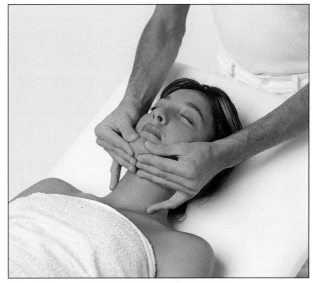

ABDOMEN AND CHEST MASSAGE

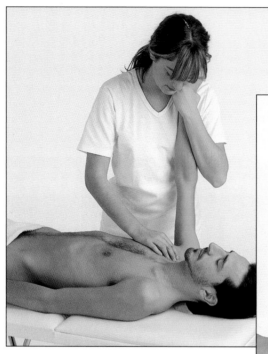

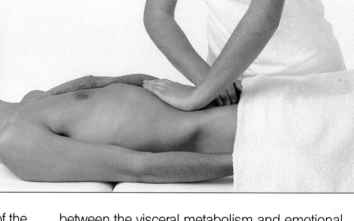

Abdomen massage can cure *blemishes* caused by *adipose deposits* and may also help resolve intestinal problems such as *constipation*, but experience and great sensitivity is needed here to avoid causing disturbance to the internal organs of the abdomen which, in fact, is not protected by hard parts, but only by abdominal muscles which in themselves are not usually very resistant.

Carry out circular stroking (clockwise so as to help *peristalsis*), drainage in the direction of the neck and of the armpits, light friction and superficial kneading of the skin and the subcutaneous area, and localized vibrations.

Avoid all kinds of percussion. Do not massage the groin, and postpone the treatment should the internal organs be inflamed.

The abdomen is the center of the body and is the place where energy stores are produced and preserved; deep in the abdomen and toward the center is the *solar plexus*. It is a very important neurovegetative center which controls relations between the visceral metabolism and emotional displays.

Bear in mind the fact that touching the abdomen is like intruding upon someone's privacy.

Chest massage is a natural ending for body front massage.

But contrary to what is generally believed, massaging the breast is not advisable because this organ is a gland.

A sagging breast or one prone to stretch marks benefits more from semicold showers than from massage, and the latter should be limited itself to gentle stroking while applying cosmetic creams.

It is instead important to massage well the pectoral muscles, often so shortened and stiff as to cause the well-known posture of curved and hunched shoulders.

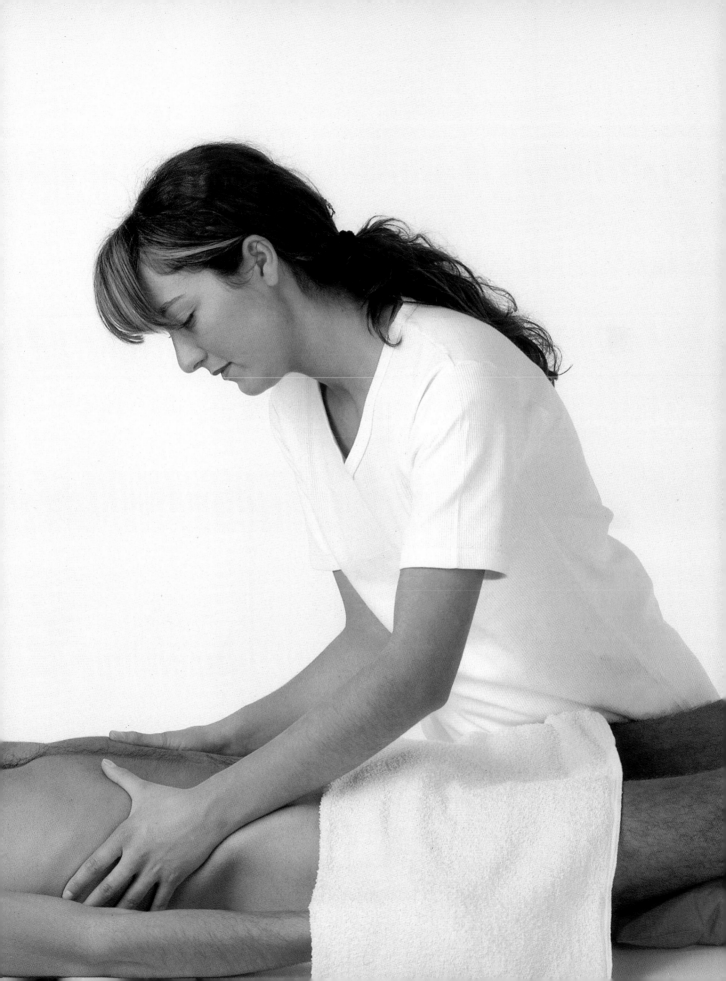

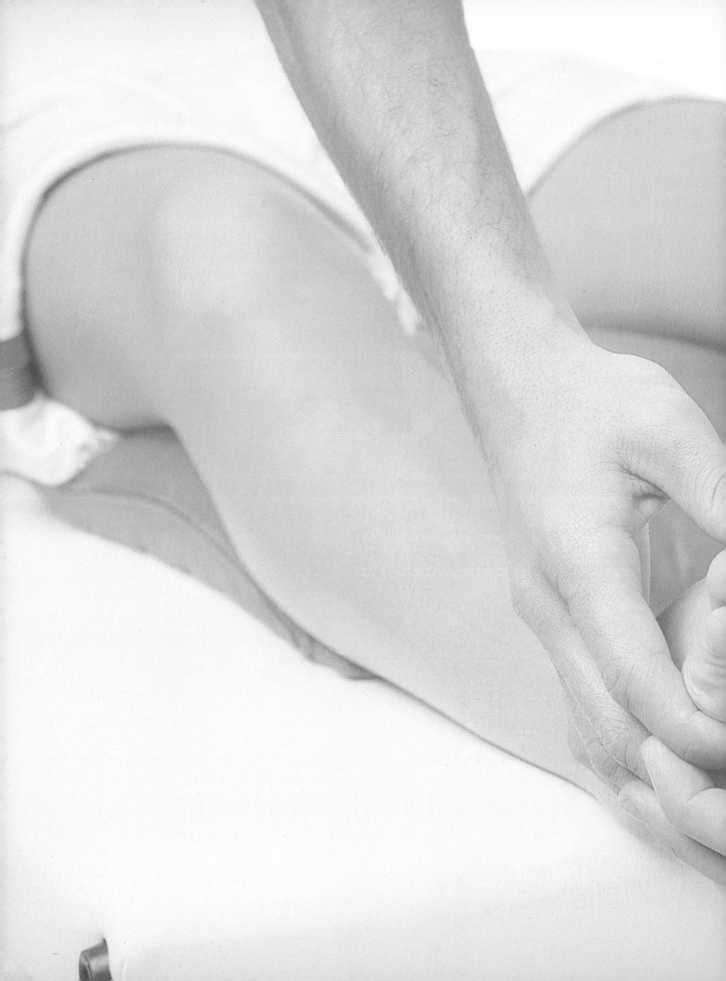

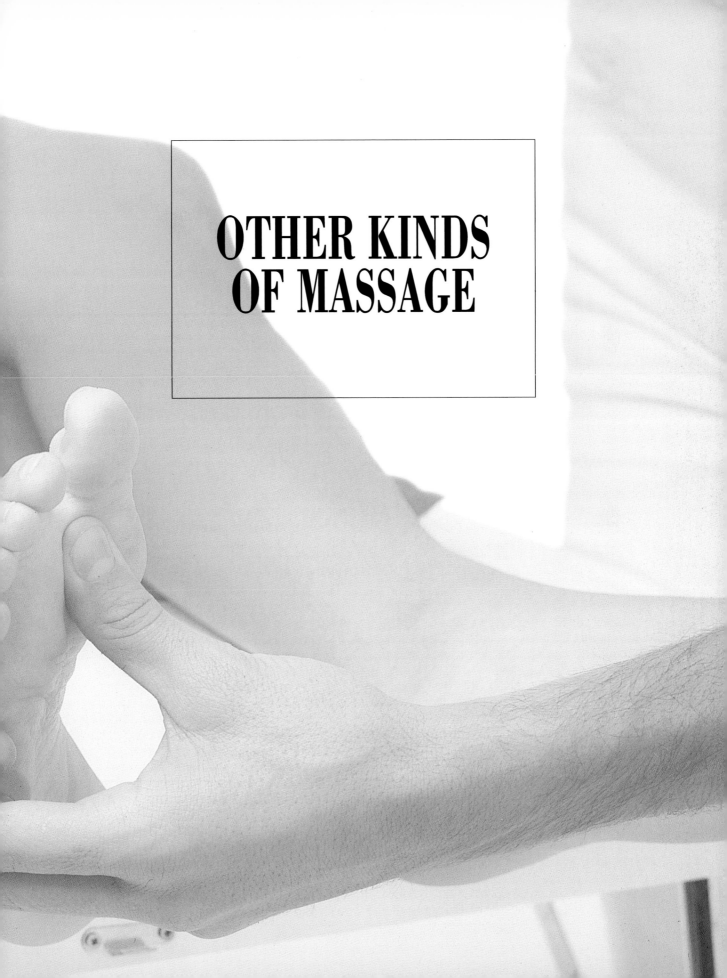

OTHER KINDS
OF MASSAGE

REFLEXOLOGY

The whole body surface is the seat of *reflex points*, on which it is possible to act in order to alleviate pain and tension (see the section on Anatomy). There are, however, regions in which nerve endings are more concentrated. These are situated at the extremities of the body: at the feet, the hands, the ears, and also on the nose. In these same areas the *meridians* of acupuncture points have their beginnings or ends and are therefore often used to rebalance energy by the insertion of needles. Studies in reflexology have resulted in *maps* being drawn up of the reflex points of the feet, the hands, and the head. These constitute a guideline, a general indication for establishing the areas in which it is possible to find the reflex point for a particular organ.

We are here mainly concerned with the foot reflexology, though its technique differs but slightly from the reflex massage of the other limbs mentioned. If we observe the map of the foot's reflex points on page 69, we can see that the sole corresponds to the front part of the body while the back corresponds to the posterior part. The *medial* area of the foot (that which runs from the big toe to the heel) corresponds to the body's midline while the *lateral* part (from the fifth toe to the heel) corresponds to the side area of the body. The *distal* part of the foot (the toes and the forefoot) correspond to the body's upper region (head, chest, and arms); the central part of the foot corresponds to the trunk and its internal organs; the *proximal* part (ankle and heel) corresponds to the body's lower region (pelvis and legs).

Paired and symmetrical organs are represented on the foot according to the relevant position (the left kidney on the left foot, the right kidney on the right foot). Dissimilar and asymmetrical organs are represented on the foot only on the side corresponding to their position (the liver only on the right foot). Finally, dissimilar but symmetrical organs are represented in a medial position on both feet (the bladder is represented half on the right foot and half on the left). The heart is represented only on the left foot. Obviously a knowledge of anatomy makes it easier for the therapist to trace a particular reflex point on the foot, but if you carry out the suggested exercises keeping in mind the map of the reflex points and also a general anatomical map of the human body, you will learn to recognize the corresponding points in a short time.

TECHNIQUE

In order to stimulate reflex action in the foot, use the tips and pads of the fingers, particularly of the thumb, as well as the knuckles, the palm of the hand, or special instruments of wood, stone, or copper more or less pointed in shape. At the beginning, use light, superficial, and widespread pressure. Later, it becomes more and more intense, deeper and specific until you reach the level of bone and the complex joint structures characteristic of the foot. It is good practice, particularly during the first treatment, to massage gently and pleasantly, making sure not to trigger acutely painful reactions. These could result in a reflex action of the vegetative nervous system bringing about nausea, vomiting, and dizziness, a sudden decrease in blood pressure, or a headache. As the treatment proceeds, and the foot becomes more flexible, pressure can be increased, arriving at a sensation somewhere between pleasure and pain. At the end of the treatment, this sensation is manifested in a pleasant feeling of lightness, and the patient "is aware" of these new feet. The treatment lasts for about 30 minutes. Repeat the treatment on alternate days for at least ten sittings. It would help to keep notes on these treatments to monitor your partner's reactions. On page 1 you could write comments after each sitting, and on the second page you might keep a picture of a foot and mark the painful spots with a circle or an x. Check the results obtained during the following treatments.

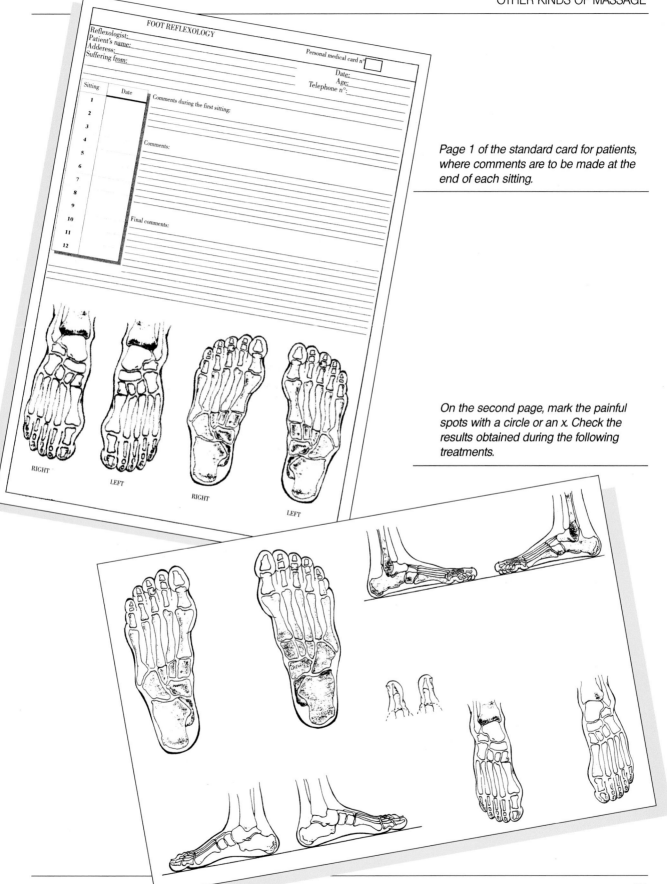

FOOT REFLEXOLOGY

Reflexologist:
Patient's name:
Adderess:
Suffering from:

Personal medical card n°

Date:
Age:
Telephone n°:

Sitting	Date
1	
2	
3	
4	
5	
6	
7	
8	
9	
10	
11	
12	

Comments during the first sitting:

Comments:

Final comments:

RIGHT

LEFT

RIGHT

LEFT

Page 1 of the standard card for patients, where comments are to be made at the end of each sitting.

On the second page, mark the painful spots with a circle or an x. Check the results obtained during the following treatments.

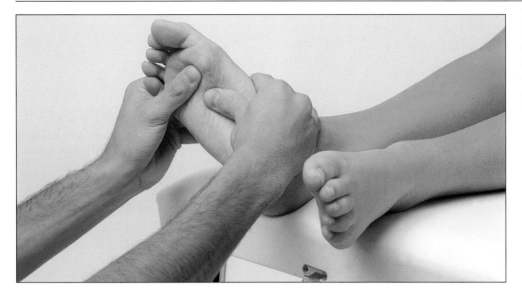

1 *The first sitting of foot reflexology should be dedicated exclusively to a diagnosis of your partner's general state of health.*

Massage at random the whole foot surface, exploring and examining each point with the palm of your hand, then with your fingertips, using slow, gentle, circular movements.

A map of foot reflexology is depicted on the opposite page. Photocopy it or make one like it, and use it to mark the points which prove most painful during treatment.

2 *Seek out on the map the points corresponding to these painful areas and check out the organs to which they refer. Give particular attention to these points during successive treatments, always bearing in mind, of course, your partner's general physiological state. For example, if your partner feels an intense pain in the area of the foot which corresponds to the bladder, a dysfunction of this organ could be presumed and treated by reflex. But we should also take into particular account the kidney and the urethra which are connected to the bladder.*

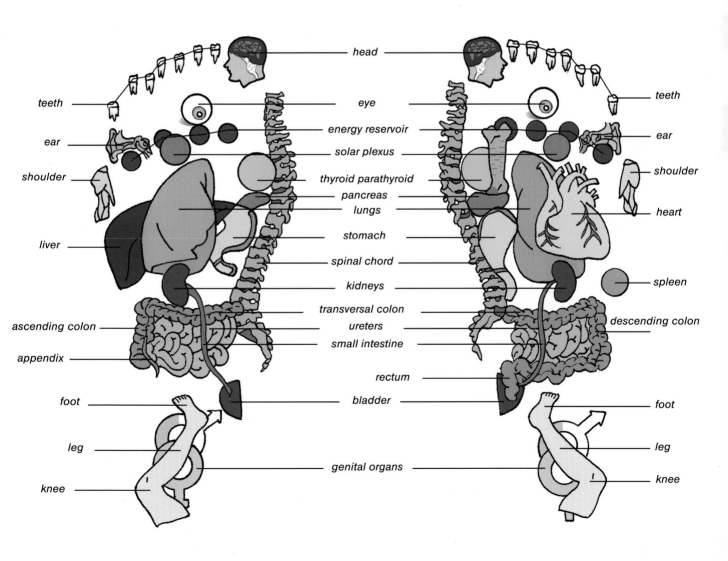

teeth · ear · shoulder · liver · ascending colon · appendix · foot · leg · knee

head · eye · energy reservoir · solar plexus · thyroid parathyroid · pancreas · lungs · stomach · spinal chord · kidneys · transversal colon · ureters · small intestine · rectum · bladder · genital organs

teeth · ear · shoulder · heart · spleen · descending colon · foot · leg · knee

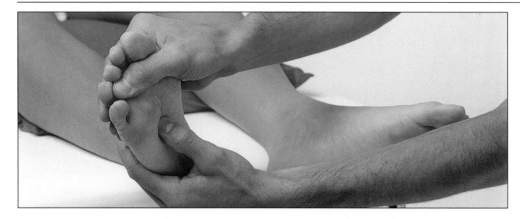

3 Cover one by one the particular areas of the foot, endeavoring to affect by reflex the various organs or muscle groups: the stomach,

the intestine,

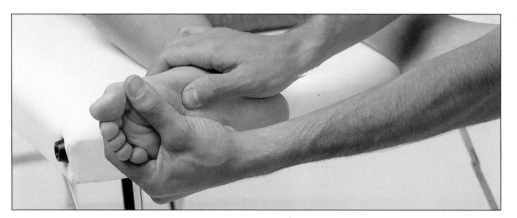

and the spine.

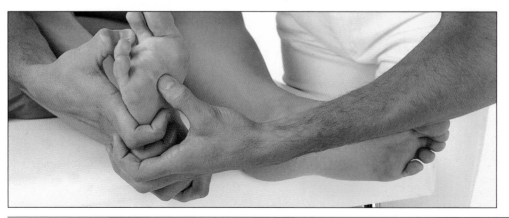

To pinpoint the solar plexus, you extend the third toe on the forefoot and locate the point of greatest bone protuberance. Immediately beneath is the maximum reflex point of the solar plexus, and it is almost always sore.

4 *When you feel confident enough, try to analyze the massage, particularly exploring the joints with your fingertips, if your partner's foot permits this. You will gradually develop the ability to "feel" the foot's response and to adapt treatment to your partner's general state of health.*

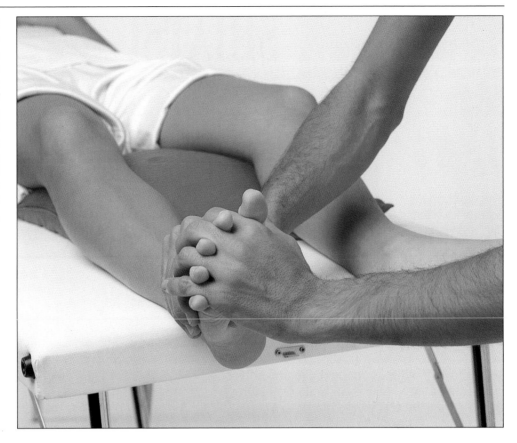

SOME DON'TS

Never overdo stimulation and do not cause pain. Massage carefully on the points corresponding to the solar plexus, the heart, and all the internal organs from which your partner suffers in any way.

WHEN ADVISABLE AND WHEN NOT ADVISABLE

Zonal massage, unlike Swedish, produces powerful reflex effects on the body and in this sense is like Shiatsu. Foot reflexology is also an excellent treatment for the health of the foot and helps prevent the damage caused by footwear and by prolonged standing.

TO CONCLUDE

Like all reflex-oriented therapies, zonal massage requires both commitment and intuition. There are several schools of reflexology which propose different techniques. The method set out in this manual is simple, pleasant, and effective, but nothing should prevent you trying new techniques. Always remember to respect the general principle that you should first do no harm.

SHIATSU

The word *Shiatsu* comes from the Japanese *shi* meaning fingers and *atzu* meaning pressure. This technique, therefore, consists in exerting pressure on certain parts of the body, which correspond to those used in acupuncture. Shiatsu, in fact, is none other than a manual technique of acupuncture and shares with it the philosophy and methods of treatments typical of Eastern medicine. According to ancient doctors and philosophers, the human body is crossed by energetic currents which follow specific channels called *meridians.* These are mainly divided into *Yin* and *Yang.*

Yin and Yang are opposites of a like energy: Yin is the female current, the dark side, sensitivity, flexibility. Yang instead represents the male element, the light side, strength, rigidity. There are no absolutes in the Yin and Yang concept, and it is believed that although opposites, these forces also work in harmony. Yang always contains a certain amount of Yin and Yin a certain amount of Yang. Men and women, in fact, possess, in different percentages, both male and female hormones. When one of the two energies increases too much it changes into its opposite. Let's take water, which is a Yin energy, as an example: as it gets cooler, water becomes more and more Yin, until it becomes ice, which is Yang.

The human being is seen as being subjected to the law of *Tao,* and its health is dependent on the balance between the crossing of the forces Yin

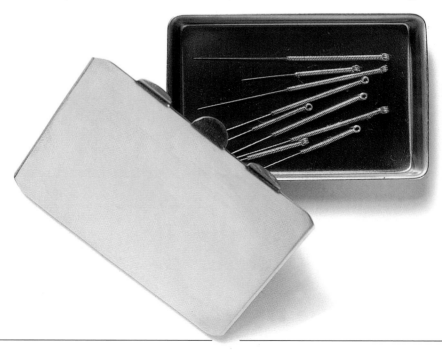

and Yang; when this balance breaks, illness sets in. Shiatsu treatment is therefore mainly preventive and consists in maintaining the body in harmonious balance. Should there no longer be harmony, it must be restored.

A total of 657 points have been identified on the human body. Joined together they form 12 meridians for each side of the body, plus another 2 which go through the center, both for the front and the back. These points, which have been scientifically established, offer less resistance to the passing of energy, and the *meridian map* that they form shows some correspondence to those channels of the circulatory system, the nervous system, the endocrine system, reproductive system, and so forth. When one of these meridians is blocked, interrupting the energy flow and breaking the harmony, the acupuncturist intervenes with very fine needles inserted in the corresponding congested area and unblocks and restores the energy flow. Shiatsu originates from a combination of the techniques that make up acupuncture and the traditional Eastern massage called *Amma* (*Am*=to press; *ma*=to stroke). Amma used to consist merely in pressing and stroking the sore areas with the fingers or the palm of the hands.

Later it was discovered that pressing and stroking the acupuncture points gave better results. This gave rise to Shiatsu.

TECHNIQUE

Shiatsu is performed mainly with the thumbs, but also with the other fingers, with the palm of the hand, with the elbow, or with the feet. It is best to treat with your partner on the floor, lying on a mattress or on a folded blanket. The arms of the therapist must be perpendicular to the point of pressure. Shiatsu is performed using the weight of the body and keeping the arms rigid: fingers and palms are therefore the means through which the energy of the therapist's body weight is transmitted to the patient. Pressure should be exerted slowly and gradually, synchronized with breathing in (synchronize your breathing with that of your partner before treatment) and breathing out. Pressure on every point should last a total of about 6 seconds, and it is a sign of expertise when the patient is unaware of the passage from heavy to light pressure. The amount of pressure exerted varies according to the points involved and to the state of health of the patient.

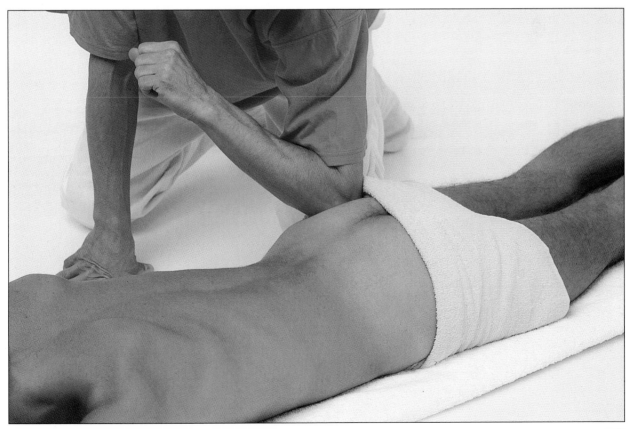

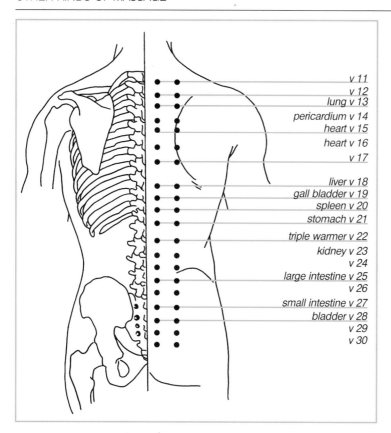

v 11
v 12
lung v 13
pericardium v 14
heart v 15
heart v 16
v 17

liver v 18
gall bladder v 19
spleen v 20
stomach v 21
triple warmer v 22
kidney v 23
v 24
large intestine v 25
v 26
small intestine v 27
bladder v 28
v 29
v 30

SHU

In order to perform Shiatsu, according to acupuncture criteria, and to act on the energy flow in a specific manner, at least ten years apprenticeship with an acupuncture expert is needed. We shall therefore limit ourselves to a treatment for rebalancing general energy, aimed mainly at relaxing muscles and creating a general sense of well-being.

The most important points to work on for this type of treatment are found on the back, and run from the sacrum to the base of the skull on both sides of the spinal column. These points correspond to the bladder meridian whose function is to check the balance of all the other meridians. The inner meridian has more of a physical effect, while the outer meridian mainly influences mental and emotional states.

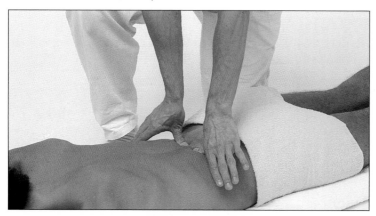

1 *Kneel behind your partner, who is in a prone position with a cushion supporting the feet. Press the inner bladder meridian, starting from the sacrum moving up the base of the neck. Move your body weight forward, transferring the pressure to your fingertips through your arms which you are holding out straight and rigid. Press while your partner is breathing in and let go while he is breathing out. The points are situated on the paravertebral muscles, immediately next to the spinal column (about 1-2 cm) and are 1-2 cm apart from each other: each point corresponds to a nerve ending from the intervertebral space.*

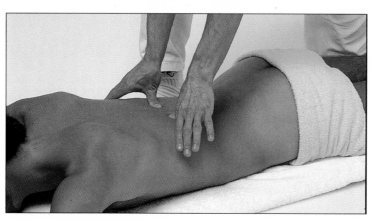

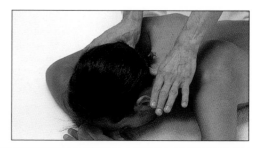

2 *Repeat this procedure on the outer bladder meridian which is situated about 2 cm from the inner meridian. There are fewer Shu points on the outer bladder meridian compared to those on the inner meridian, but we will treat them both alike so as to avoid confusion.*

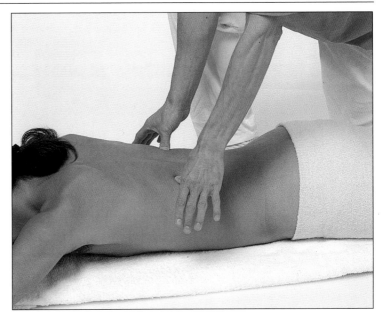

DU MAI

Du Mai is another important meridian situated on the back, as it governs all the Yang meridians. Du Mai is the central posterior meridian, and its anterior equivalent is *Ren Mai*, which is instead responsible for all Yin meridians. The *Du Mai* points are situated in the spaces between one vertebra and another. To pinpoint them, identify the spinal processes of two adjacent vertebrae: the space that divides them corresponds to a *Du Mai* point.

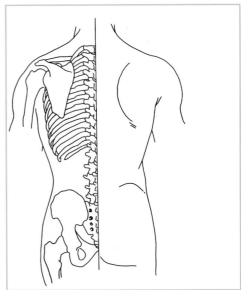

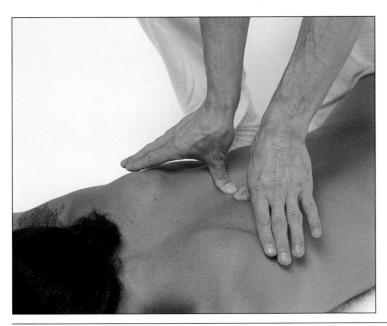

3 *Treat the Du Mai points starting from the sacrum, moving from one vertebra to the next until you reach the base of the skull. Treat each point with the pad of both thumbs. The direction of the thrust, as can be seen in the picture, aims toward the middle of the body, with the tip of both thumbs touching each other at the end.*

Exercises 1, 2, and 3 are in themselves an excellent relaxation treatment and should be carried out at the beginning of each Shiatsu sitting. You may also introduce this sequence of movements before starting other massage techniques in order to relax your partner and increase the effectiveness of treatment.

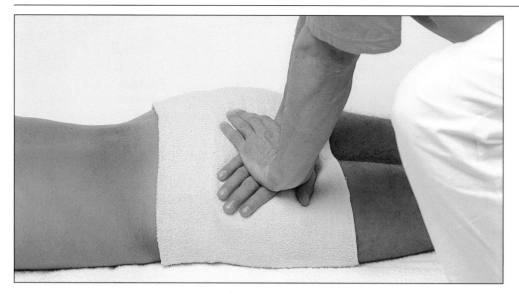

LEGS

4 *Kneel at the side of your partner's leg. With superimposed hands exert pressure on the sacrum,*

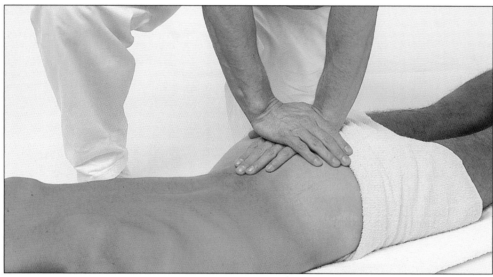

the buttocks,

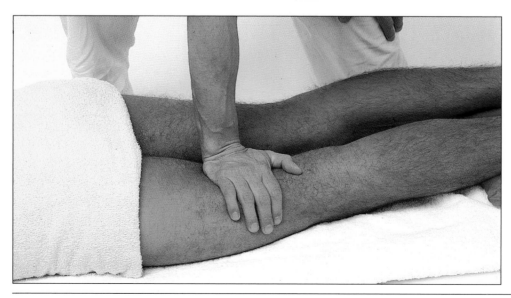

and the leg.

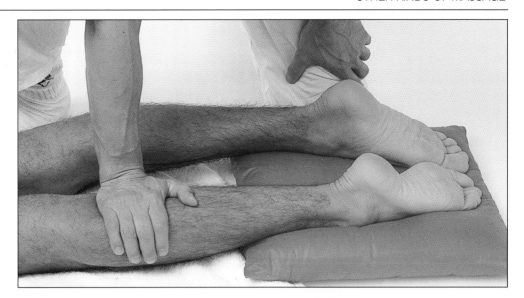

Move by a hand's width toward the foot,

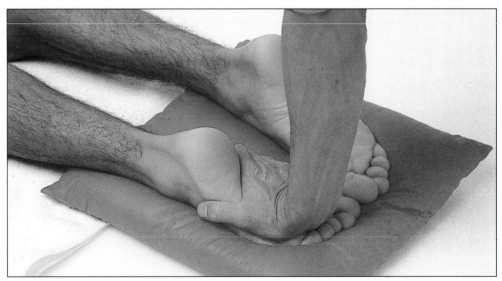

until reaching the sole of the foot.

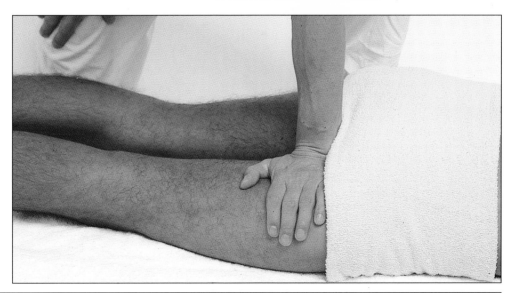

5 *Repeat on the other leg.*

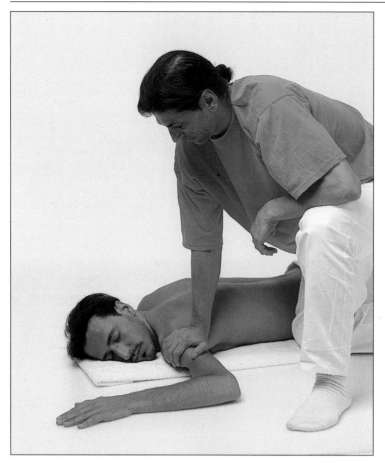

ARMS

6 *Repeat the above on the arm, starting from the shoulder.*

Move by a hand's width toward the hand.

Exert pressure on the hand and then repeat on the other arm.

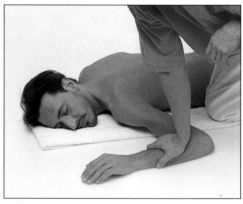

7 *Repeat the exercise on the upper and lower limbs, this time with your partner lying supine.*

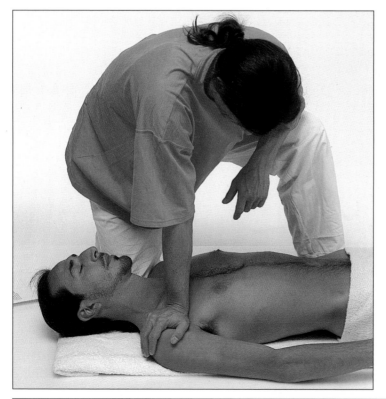

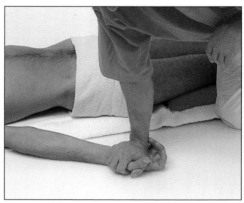

8 *The front of the body is more delicate and sensitive (Yin), so you must therefore exert a gentler pressure here. There are many important and delicate points on the abdomen and chest. Try massaging them and discuss impressions with your partner.*

9 *There are many important acupuncture points on the face too. Press gently, combining a slow circular motion with the tips of the thumbs, making sure to avoid causing pain.*

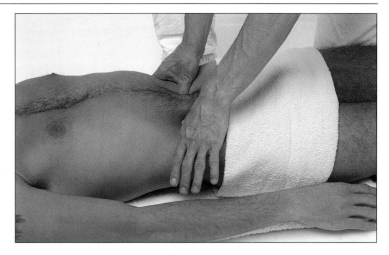

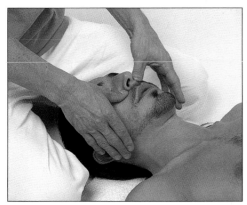

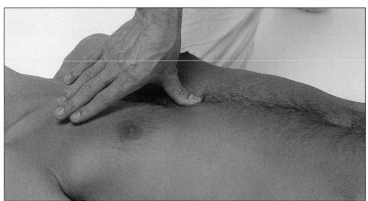

SOME DON'TS

Do not press with your fingertips, but with the fleshy part of your finger pads. Performing Shiatsu does not involve physical effort but a correct use of energy. Press without effort but use your body weight. Do not press too hard, especially on the joints and in the vicinity of delicate internal organs. Pressure should not be jerky but instead should be gentle and slow. Ease off slowly and gently.

WHEN ADVISABLE

Shiatsu is advised for all psychosomatic disorders that are not yet pathological. When a condition becomes organic, it is too late to intervene and correct the energy imbalance. Shiatsu is very effective in cases of physical and emotional tension and is an extremely effective treatment for relaxation. As with all therapies of an energetic nature, Shiatsu restores the body's general balance, but also gives back tone and energy to those organs deficient in them.

WHEN NOT ADVISABLE

Shiatsu must not be performed on people with febrile conditions or those susceptible to internal hemorrhages, ulcers, or fractures. Furthermore, it is not advisable on pregnant women or during the menstrual period. Avoid performing Shiatsu on others if you yourself are in an agitated state or during natural phenomena which involve the universe's energies (of which our body is a smaller version) such as storms, eclipses, and earthquakes.

TO CONCLUDE

Performing Shiatsu is not simple: be patient and use all your sensitivity to perceive when you're operating correctly. Never perform more than three Shiatsu treatments a day because, as you will see for yourself, contact with other energies for a prolonged period of time may leave you in a state of confusion and torpor. Always work barefooted and have a shower at the end of each treatment.

SHIATSU POINTS

With the help of your own sensitivity and intuition, find out for yourself where your partner's Shiatsu points are. Concentrate on the hollows of the body, on those places where your thumb's pads easily adapt themselves to the shape of the structures below the skin. In time, you will learn to perceive the *Empty* and *Full* energy zones, and your body will discover how to adapt to your partner's responses. Relax, breathe deeply, and keep your mind empty and your perception vigilant: it will take time, but you will eventually acquire the ability to perceive even the smallest of energy changes.

THE NAPE

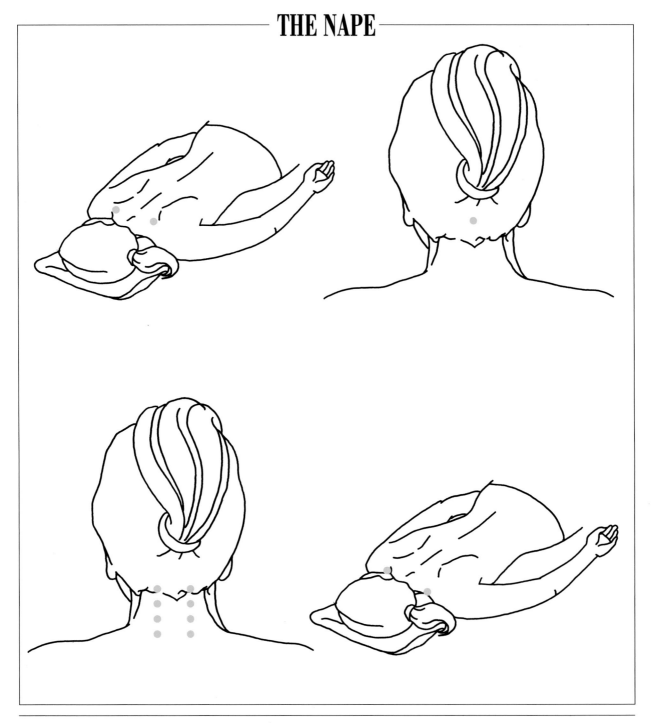

THE BACK

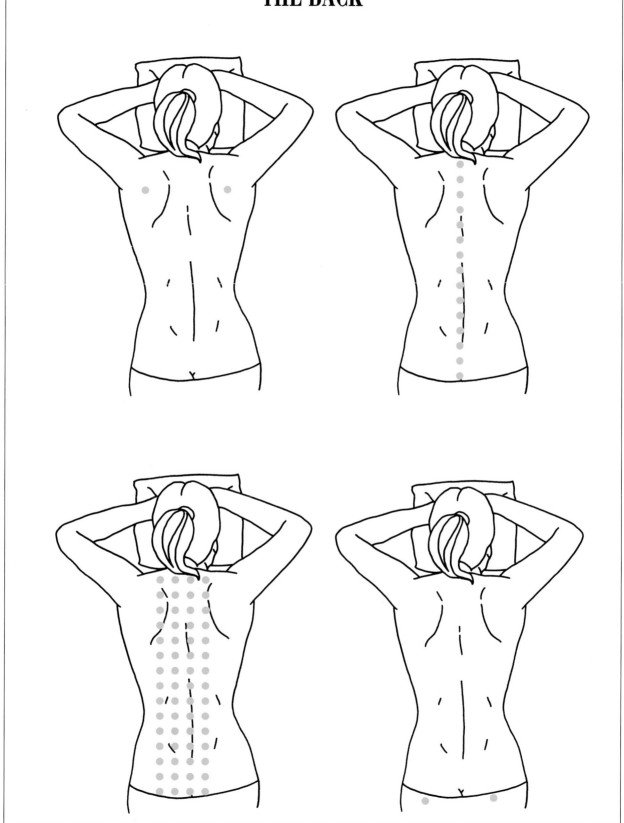

THE LEGS AND FEET

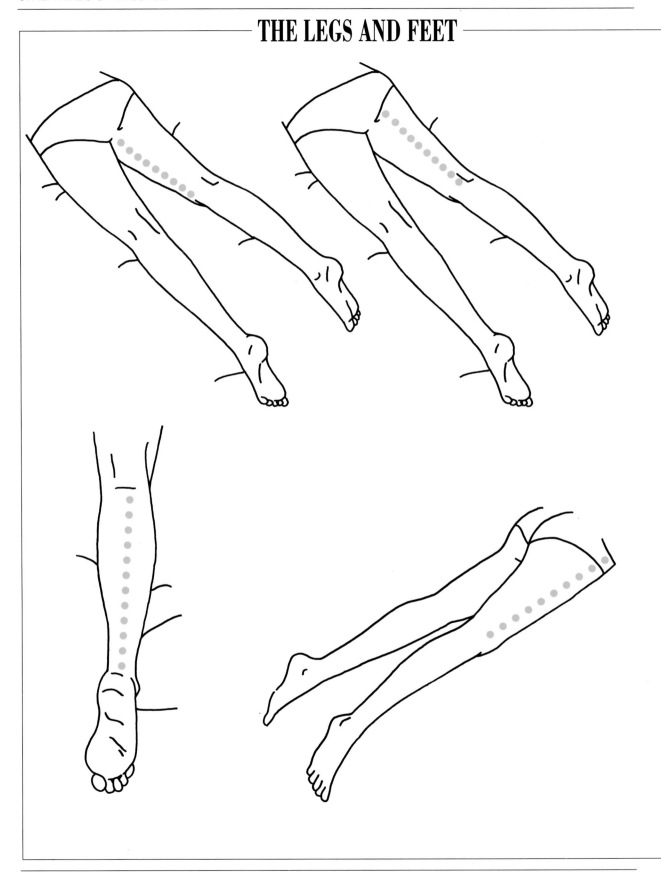

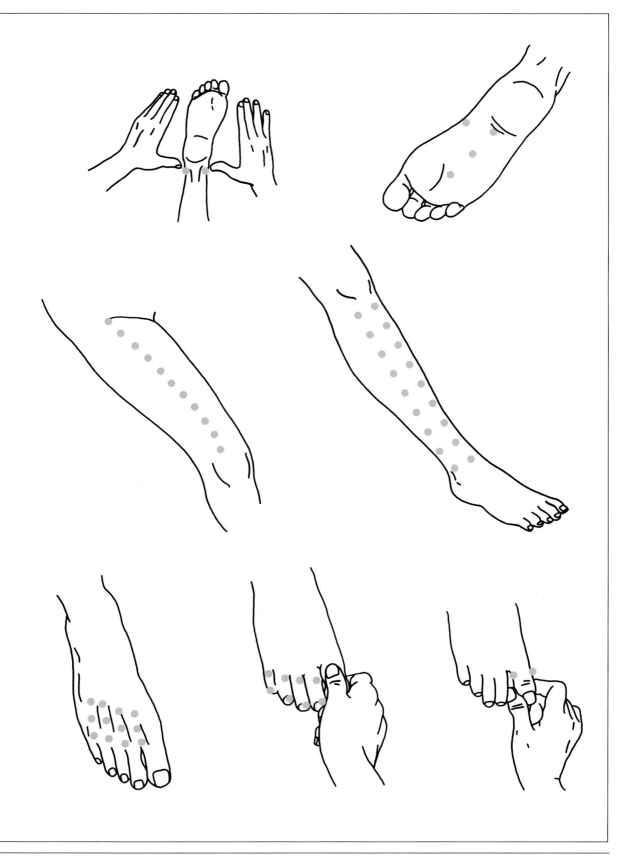

THE ARMS AND HANDS

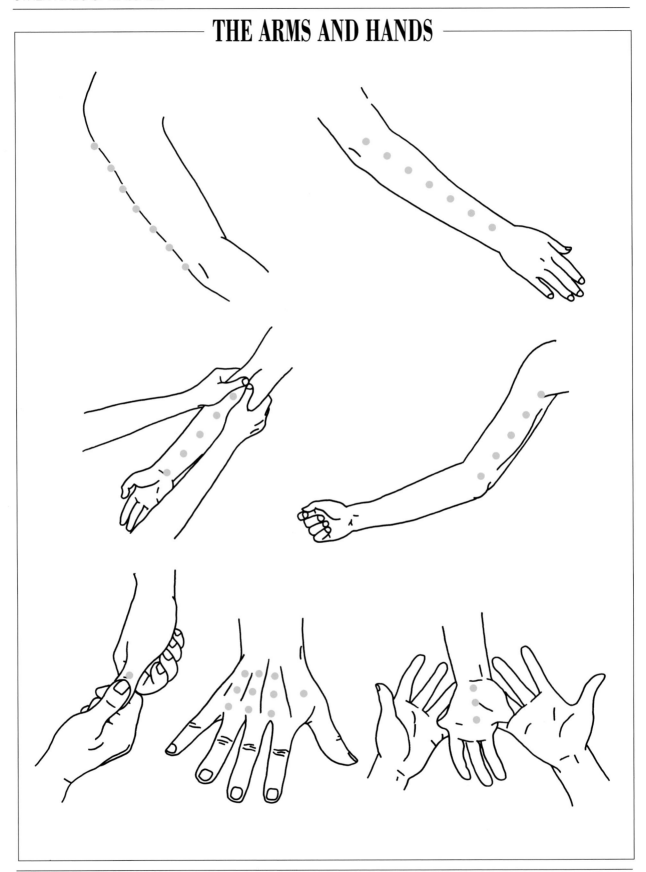

THE HEAD, FACE, AND NECK

CONNECTIVE TISSUE MASSAGE

THE STORY OF AN INTUITION

Connective tissue massage was discovered casually in 1929 by Elisabeth Dike, thanks to a disease she had been suffering for years. Her lower right leg suffered from serious circulation problems and at that time amputation appeared to be the only therapy possible. Ms Dike also suffered from pains in the lumbar region and tried to alleviate the pain through digital tractions in the lumbosacral region. To her great surprise, she noticed that thanks to this treatment, the leg had begun to get better. Following this discovery, the technique of connective tissue massage was born and perfected, but it was not until later that its effects on the body were studied. At the beginning, in fact, the medical class, having failed to find a scientific reason for the results that were being obtained, was rather skeptical. It wasn't until further discoveries were made in the field of neurophysiology that the technique was approved by official medical authorities.

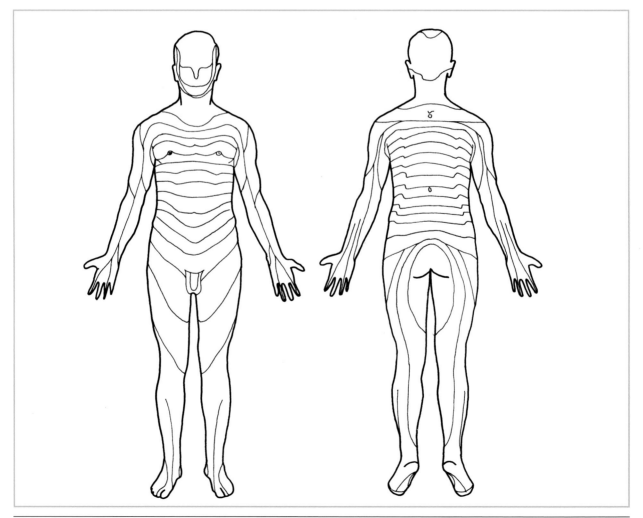

THE DEEP AND REFLEXIVE EFFECT OF CONNECTIVE TISSUE MASSAGE

As already seen in the chapter on Anatomy, recent neurological studies on the body's innervation system have revealed a division of zones of the body, in which each nerve corresponds to a segment of the spinal chord which innervates it. Each *neurotome* (nerve plexus along the spinal column) is connected to specific internal organs (*enterotomes*), to specific muscles (*myotomes*) and to a specific surface of the epidermis (*dermatome*). Any kind of functional alteration with one of these systems is reflected in the connecting systems through the neurotome. The result is that a muscular problem, or one concerning an internal organ, manifests itself in a specific area of the body. Furthermore, stimulation on the part of the skin concerned provokes a reflexive effect in the corresponding muscles and internal organs, thus positively influencing on the course of the illness. *Maps of the body surface* showing the zones corresponding to each of internal organs and specific muscles have been drawn after the study of these relationships.

TECHNIQUE

This technique is performed with the tips of the third and fourth finger, which move the skin and lift it above the underlying connective tissue. The fingers may be either flat or perpendicular to the patient's body surface, depending on whether superficial or deep stimulation is required. The patient's health conditions and responsiveness determine the depth of stimulation practiced. The patient is usually seated on a stool, but it is also possible to perform the treatment on someone in a prone, supine, or side-lying position, should that person be unable to remain seated for long.

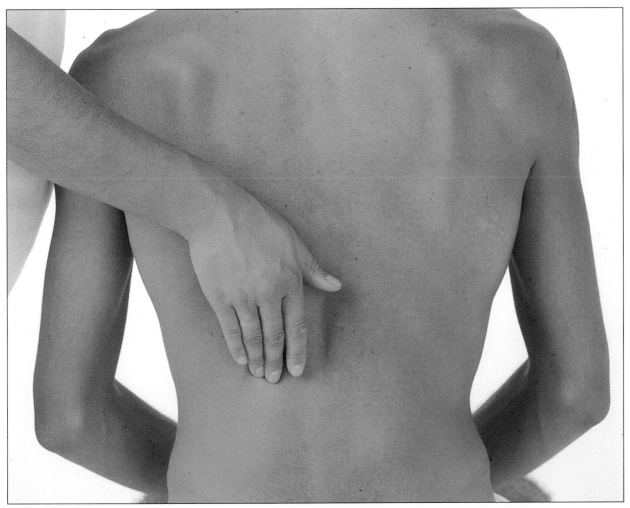

DIFFERENT PHASES

Ms Dike's experience has shown that it is preferable, during treatment, to use certain techniques to achieve maximum results and avoid exaggerated and unpleasant neurovegetative reactions in the patient.

The first phase of the treatment deals with what is called the *preparatory work* (see pictures 1 and 2). This first treatment sitting is needed in order to evaluate your partner's reactions and to decide on a treatment program. Should there be excessive reactions at this phase, interrupt treatment for a week and then attempt a similar sitting.

Preparatory work is followed by a series of additional tractions, worked out on the basis of types of problems being faced. They are used to alleviate muscle tension in the regions to be treated. To the above-mentioned tractions are added, at every sitting, *additional tractions* that follow a specific pattern, dictated by experience,

and which together form the first, second, and third therapeutic series. However, the treatment works progressively, gradually drawing closer to the area where the skin suffers most. Several sittings are often needed before the area concerned can be treated. Every sitting starts off with the basic preparation to which are added, at the following sittings, and according to the needs of the patient, the first, second or third therapeutic series, as well as accessory tractions. Should the patient have problems with his lower limbs, the practitioner should, after the initial preparation, pass directly to accessory tractions and the treatment specific to the lower limbs, gradually drawing closer to the area concerned.

It is good practice to repeat the initial preparation at intervals during a sitting and always end the treatment with it. In the pictures on the opposite page and on the following pages, the numbers indicate the sequence to be followed when performing traction.

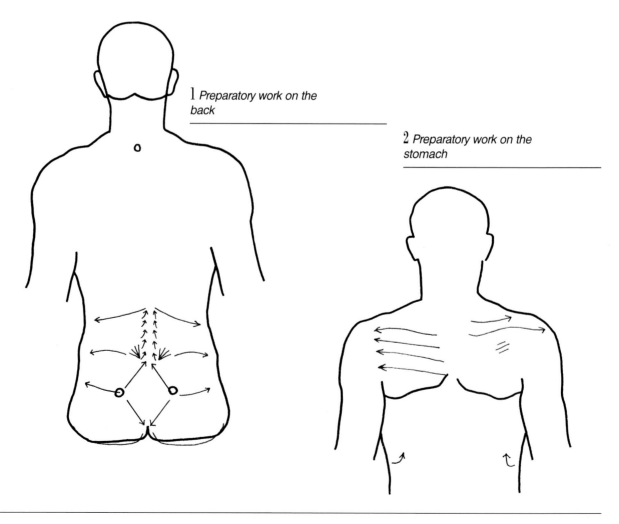

1 *Preparatory work on the back*

2 *Preparatory work on the stomach*

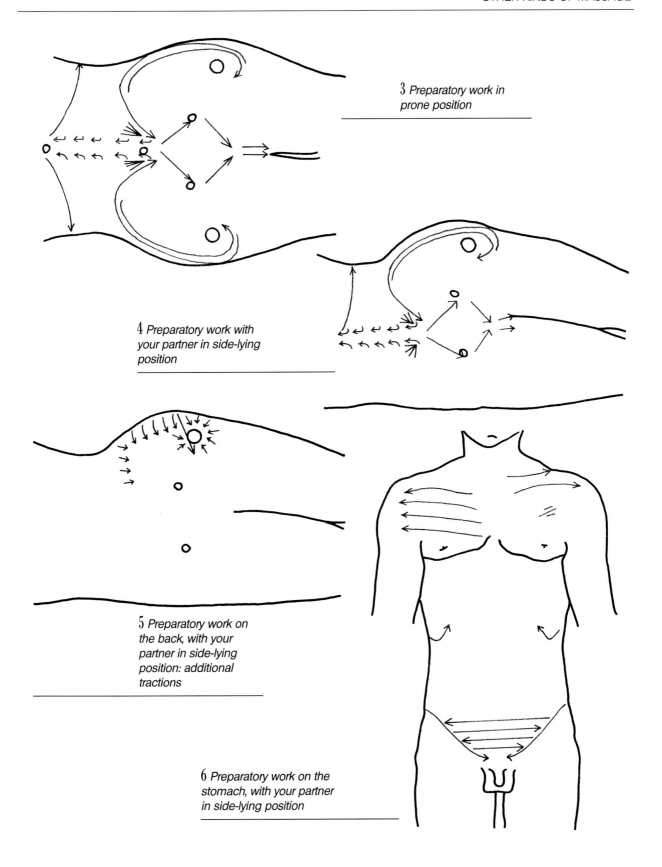

3 *Preparatory work in prone position*

4 *Preparatory work with your partner in side-lying position*

5 *Preparatory work on the back, with your partner in side-lying position: additional tractions*

6 *Preparatory work on the stomach, with your partner in side-lying position*

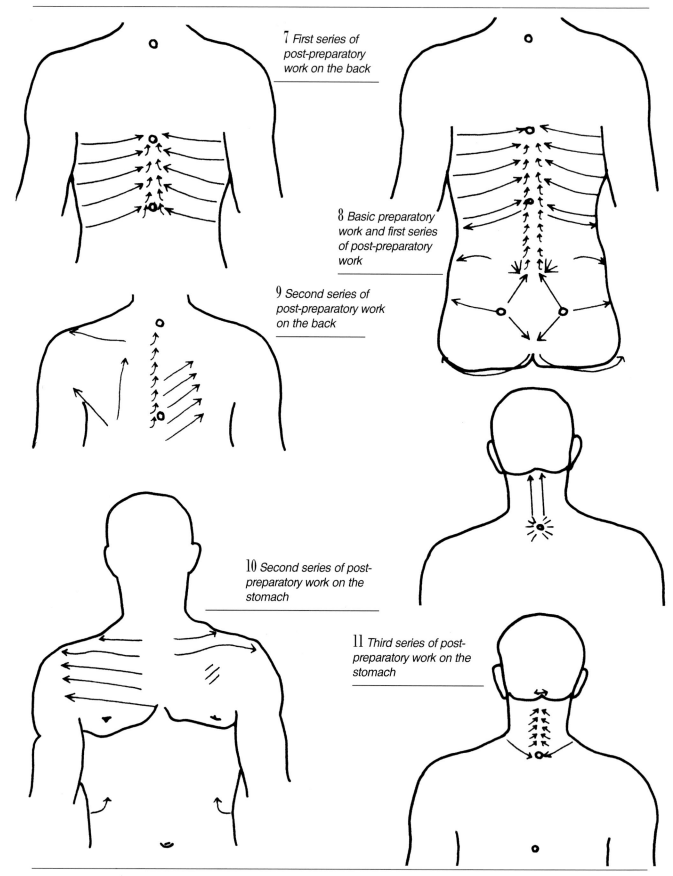

7 First series of post-preparatory work on the back

8 Basic preparatory work and first series of post-preparatory work

9 Second series of post-preparatory work on the back

10 Second series of post-preparatory work on the stomach

11 Third series of post-preparatory work on the stomach

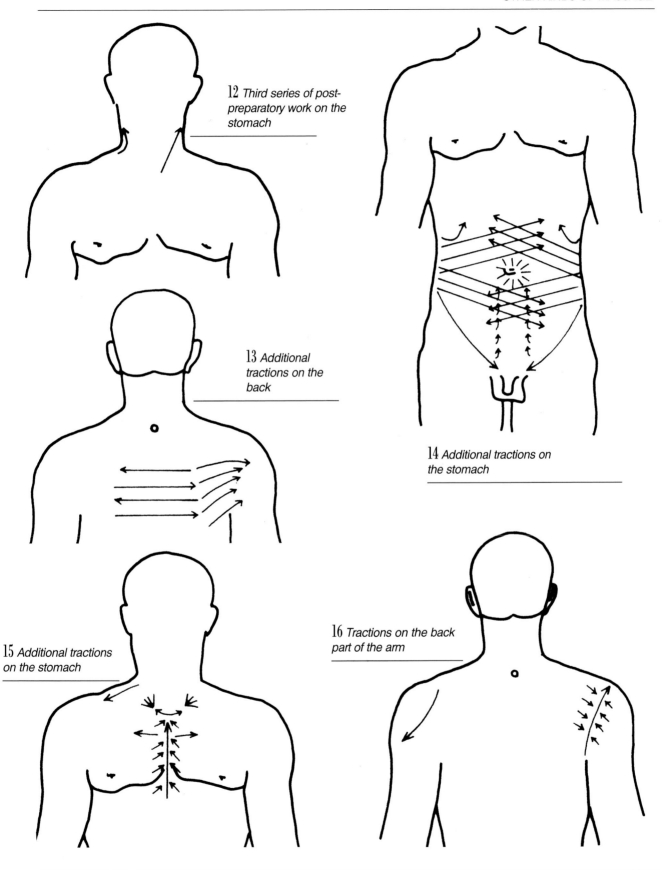

12 *Third series of post-preparatory work on the stomach*

13 *Additional tractions on the back*

14 *Additional tractions on the stomach*

15 *Additional tractions on the stomach*

16 *Tractions on the back part of the arm*

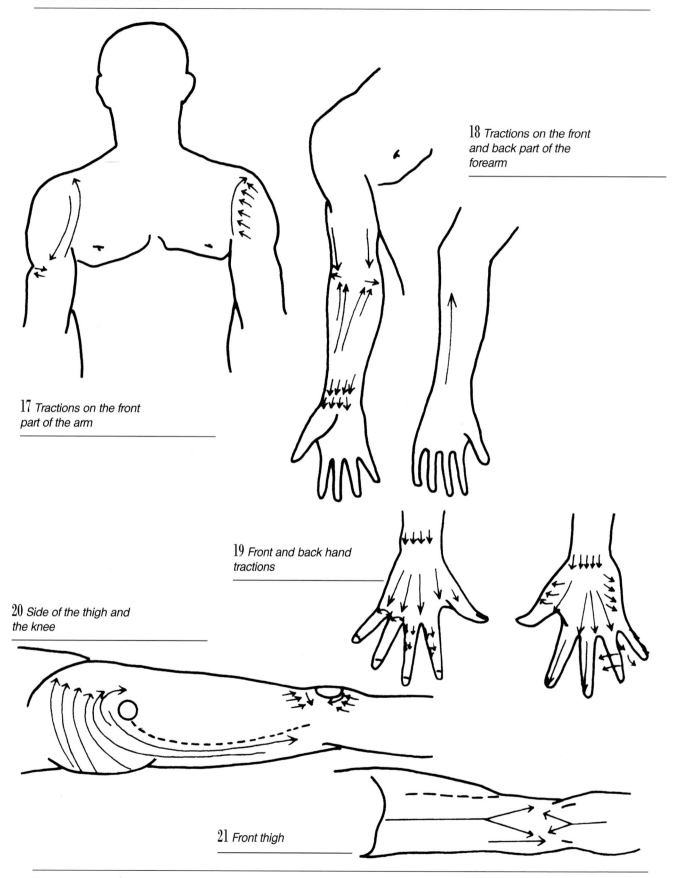

17 *Tractions on the front part of the arm*

18 *Tractions on the front and back part of the forearm*

19 *Front and back hand tractions*

20 *Side of the thigh and the knee*

21 *Front thigh*

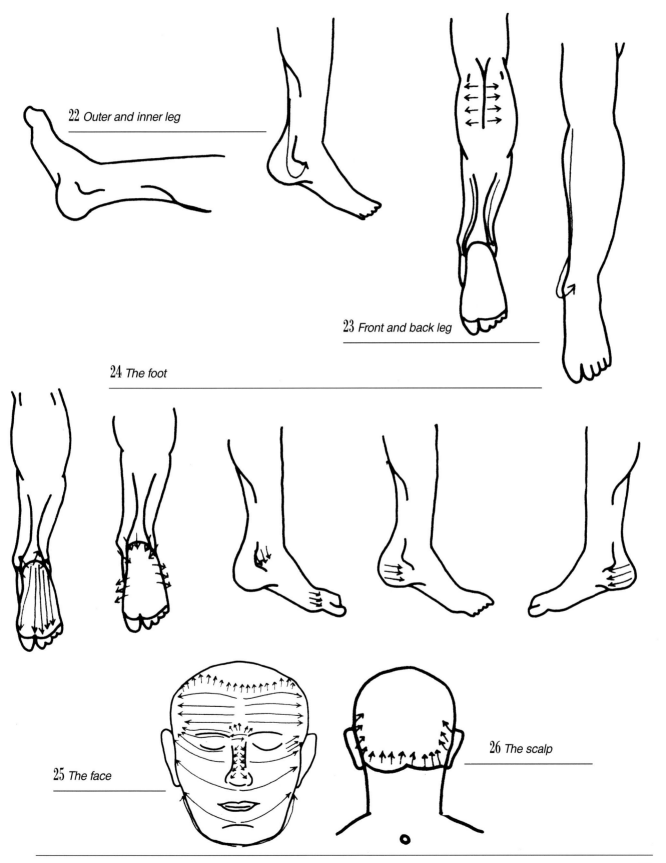

22 *Outer and inner leg*

23 *Front and back leg*

24 *The foot*

25 *The face*

26 *The scalp*

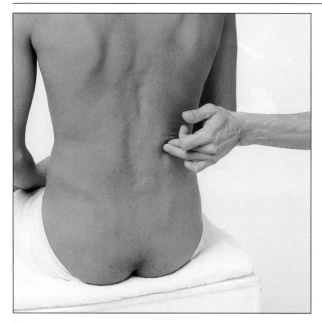

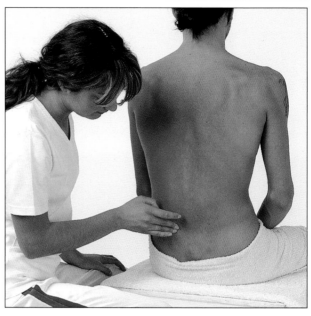

1 With your partner sitting on a stool, examine his back, performing light longitudinal tractions along the spinal column. Note where there is greatest skin adhesion to the underlying tissues, where it is most painful, and where swelling occurs.

2 Try the initial preparation (not more than twice) at first superficially and then in greater depth. Red strips will most probably appear on the treated spots: this reaction is quite common and indicates a healthy neurovegetative response to the stimulus.

3 Gradually, and spacing out the sittings, try the entire therapeutical series, the accessory tractions and the limb treatment, until you feel you have acquired enough experience.

4 Spreading it over several sittings, try a complete specific treatment, starting from the basic preparation and following the techniques suggested in the manual, gradually arriving at the part to be treated.

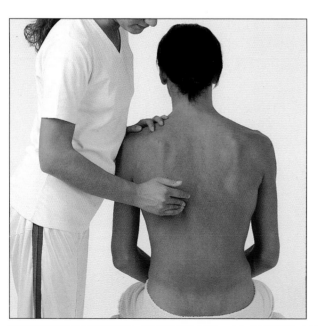

SOME DON'TS

Never overdo stimulation or cause pain. Do not forget the preparatory work at the beginning of each sitting. Use only the third and fourth fingertips, at times superimposing them in order to achieve a deeper effect, and work to traction the skin in your direction. This is effective and spares you useless efforts. Avoid uncomfortable positions – put yourself in a position suitable for your body in order to obtain best results for your partner. Do not be in a hurry and respect the patterns that have been proposed.

WHEN ADVISABLE

Connective tissue massage restores the vegetative balance of the connective tissues and has a reflex action upon the deepest layers of the body. Therefore it is advised after all acute and nearly all chronic diseases, especially after fractures, dislocations, and contractures; for people suffering from arthrosis, arthritis, limb and muscle pains, muscle rheumatism, lumbago (also in the acute phase), acute stiff neck; problems associated with scoliosis and scars; paralysis due to lesions of the peripheral nervous system; circulatory problems; in angina pectoris and heart attack; chronic cold; bronchial asthma; gastritis; liver diseases, gall bladder and billiary duct diseases; and in visceral and kidney diseases. It also can be helpful in some cases for pregnant women or sick children, although in these cases it is always best to be extremely careful, and ask your doctor's advice before intervening.

WHEN NOT ADVISABLE

Connective tissue massage is not advisable in the acute phase of most illnesses, tumoral processes, or in psychoses in their advanced phases. If your partner has problems with pressure, then perform treatment with him lying in a prone or supine position. Avoid touching inflamed areas, especially those which are tense and painful; you will be able to work on those areas in subsequent sittings, when your partner's condition has improved. If in the first sittings signs of intolerability should appear, stop for a longish period and then try again.

AN EXAMPLE OF TREATMENT

In a case of acute periarthritis of the shoulder, I would treat the patient with the preparatory work which helps to relax the back and the shoulder blade reflexively. After 2 or 3 sittings, I would start the greater preparation (preparatory work + first therapeutic series). Gradually, I would add the other therapeutic series to the treatment as well as the specific shoulder and armpit connective tissue massage. When the arm is able to move, it also would be treated, down to the elbow.

TO CONCLUDE

Connective tissue massage is a very effective technique but it requires experience and ability on the part of the practitioner. Learn to work gently and progressively to ensure that no damage will be caused to your partner but that your treatments are effective.

MANUAL LYMPHATIC DRAINAGE

Manual lymphatic drainage was discovered in the 1930s by two Danish therapists, Astrid and Emil Vodder, who were the first to have the courage to massage the *superficial lymphatic ganglia*. Since then, thanks to in-depth studies on the lymphatic system, this technique has evolved, and there exist today many schools of massage which include lymph drainage in their curricula.

THE EFFECTS OF LYMPH DRAINAGE ON LYMPHATIC CIRCULATION

The aim of lymph drainage is to help the *circulation* of the lymph and its *flow* in the blood circulation. The lymph flows from the periphery to the center of the body, gathering in groups of small cisterns in specific points of the body, both deep and superficial. It then flows into the venous circulation where the internal jugular vein and the subclavian vein meet (this area is known as *terminus*). The lymph from the left chest, the left arm, and the left half of the head and face flows into the *left terminus*, while the remaining areas of the body flow into the *right terminus*.

TECHNIQUE

In order to perform lymph drainage correctly, it is necessary to bear in mind two rules regarding lymphatic circulation:
- the lymph flows much slower than the blood, so it is therefore of the utmost importance to slow down the rhythm of the massage, performing the movements as if in slow motion. Not adhering to this one fundamental rule significantly compromises the effects of the treatment, and one risks causing the lymph to slow down further;
- before draining the lymph in a region of the body, it is always necessary to empty the superficial lymphatic ganglion into which it flows.
To make things easier, I have divided the body surface into quadrants, each of which responds to a lymphatic ganglion into which flows all the lymph of the corresponding quadrant. Drainage occurs in the direction of the lymphatic ganglion. The sequence of lymphatic drainage is not difficult to understand: first empty the lymphatic ganglion and then drain the lymph of the corresponding quadrant. The quadrants closest to the terminus must be drained before those situated further away.

To increase the effectiveness of the treatment, use delicate and decongesting oils like those scented lavender or jasmine.

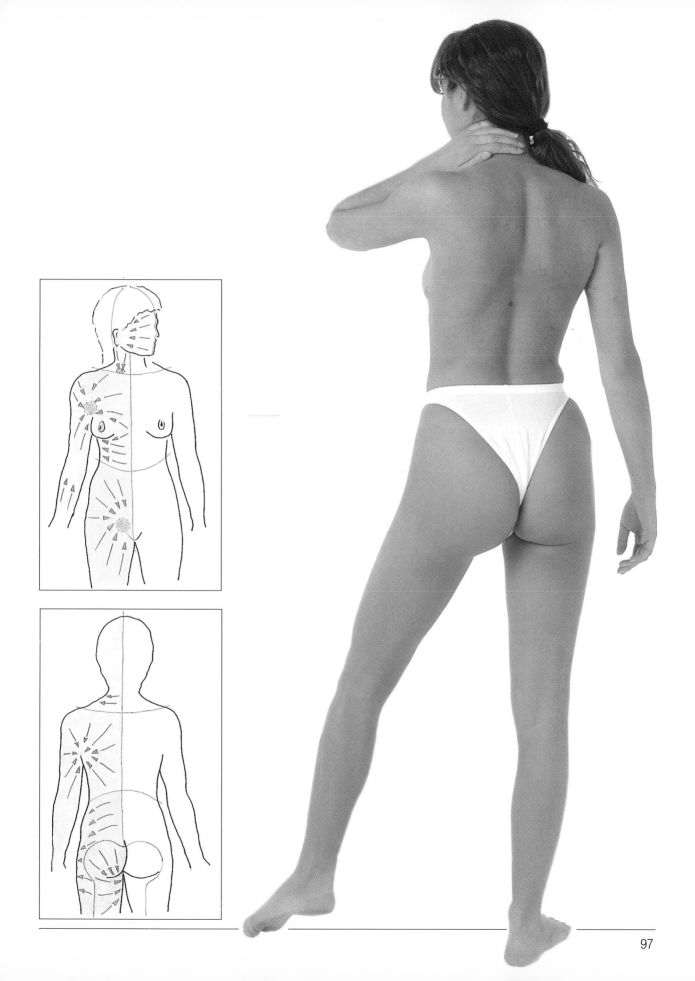

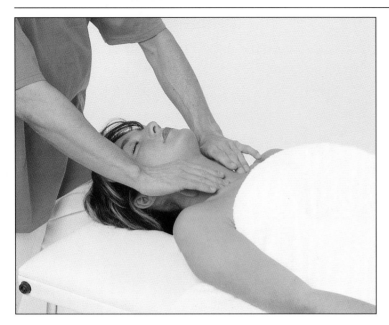

FIXED CIRCULAR MOVEMENTS

This method is performed with the fingertips gently pressing the skin and drawing ellipses; there is no movement up and down the skin and the circular motions start from the wrist. This movement allows the emptying of the superficial lymphatic ganglia, but is also used, with some variations, on the face, the head, the neck, the elbows, the knees, the hands, and the feet.

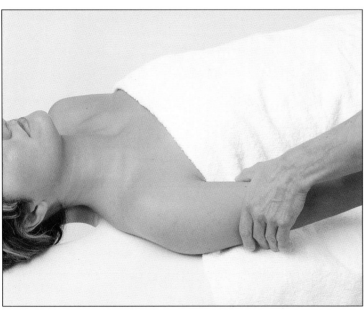

PUMPING

This movement is carried out with the whole hand covering the entire part of the body undergoing treatment and gently pushing in the direction of the drainage. The rule to be followed is that one should use minimum pressure and maximum push. This movement is performed on the arms, the legs, the thighs, and the sides of the chest (these are all curved areas easily covered by the hand). To make things easier, we shall divide the movement into four phases: put the arch formed by the thumb and the index finger on the curved part of the body to be treated; lean with the whole palm of the hand; push in the direction of the drainage without pressing with your fingertips and finally lift your hand.

Pumping and fixed circular motions are often performed together: while one hand pumps, the other is in front of it, carrying out fixed circular motions.

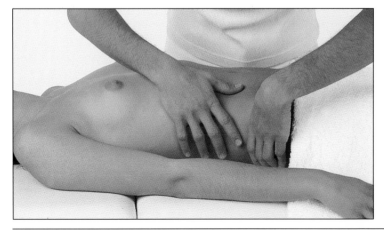

EROGATION

This is a variation of the pumping movement which involves, at the end of the movements, the fingers moving towards the outer part of the body. The erogation movement is only performed on the arms and on the legs and permits a more accurate check on the direction of the drainage.

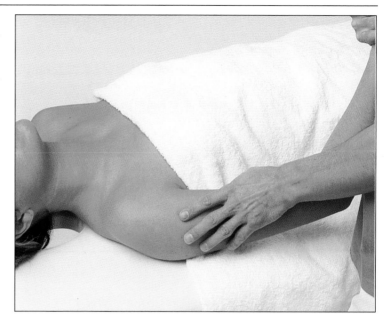

ROTATION

This movement is performed with the whole palm of the hand, with the fingers slightly open but relaxed and the thumb extended. Drainage follows the direction of the index finger. You must never press with your fingertips. At the end of the thrust, the thumb draws closer to the other fingers, and the hand is practically closed. The rotating movement is used on the large flat surfaces of the body (the stomach, the back, the chest, and the buttocks).

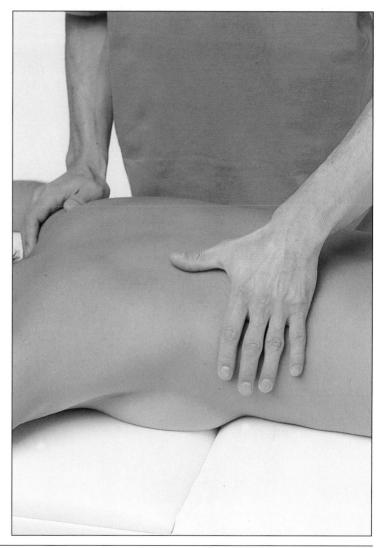

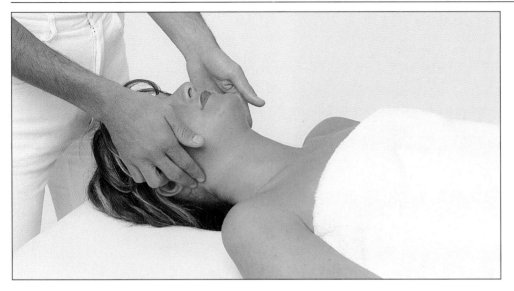

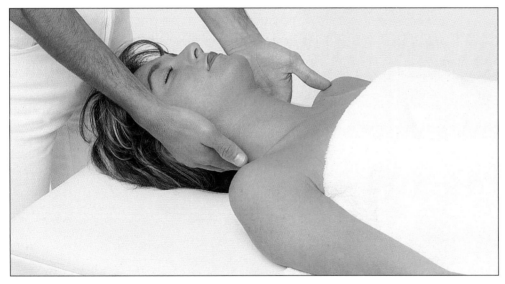

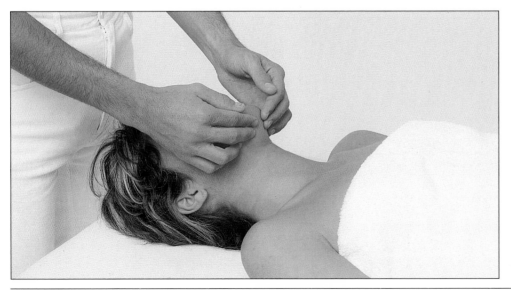

DRAINAGE OF THE NECK

This must always be performed at the beginning of each treatment.

1 *Begin by performing gentle stroking on the neck and shoulders.*

2 *Perform fixed circular motions starting from the profundus (the hollow just beneath the ear) to the terminus. Repeat from three to seven times.*

3 *Perform more fixed circular motions starting from the back part of the neck to the terminus. Repeat from three to seven times.*

4 *Repeat the same exercise, this time from the middle of the chin toward the profundus.*

5 *Carry out fixed circular motions in the preauricular and postauricular regions. Direct the thrusts toward the base of the neck. Repeat three times and then perform fixed circular motions once again from the profondus to the terminus.*

6 *Perform the same circular motions on the shoulders (deltoids), on the trapezium, and on the upper clavicular region, always in the direction of the terminus.*

7 *To conclude, massage the profundus and the terminus once again, and end the treatment with gentle stroking similar to that performed at the start of the sitting.*

DRAINAGE OF THE LEGS

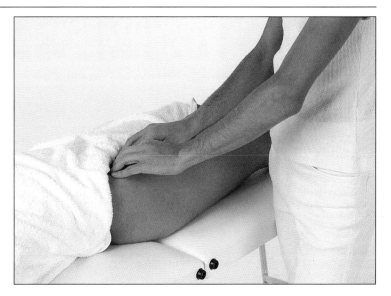

8 *After massaging the neck (exercises 1 to 7) and gently stroking the feet and groin, perform fixed circular motions on the groin lymph nodes, pushing toward the center of the groin.*

9 *Drain the inside of the thigh (extremely important), the front, and the outside of the thigh, combining pumpings and fixed circular motions.*

10 *Drain the front of the knee using the pumping technique, and then approach the side and back of the knee using fixed circular motions, pushing in the direction of the groin.*

11 *Drain the back of the leg with erogation movements, using both of your hands, and address the front of the leg by pumping. You may combine treatment of both areas of the leg by alternating the hand movements.*

12 *Treat the whole foot and the ankle with fixed circles. Light stroking from the foot to the groin will end the treatment.*

SOME DON'TS

Avoid particularly abrupt and rapid movements. Do not press too hard: remember the rule of minimum pressure and maximum push. Never forget to drain the neck first.

WHEN ADVISABLE

Manual lymphatic drainage is advised especially in cases of edema, water retention, the slowing down of the circulation in general, and the slowing down of the lymphatic circulation in particular. It is an excellent aesthetic treatment and, together with other techniques, it helps reduce cellulitis. Lymphatic drainage is effective also against acne, couperose, the premature aging of the cells, and thick scarring. In medicine, lymphatic drainage may be an excellent support therapy for disorders of rheumatic or neurological origins, such as headaches or neuralgia of the trigeminal nerve.

WHEN NOT ADVISABLE

It is not advisable to perform lymph drainage in the following cases: in patients suffering from asthma and/or with an inflamed lower stomach; patients suffering from phlebitis, thrombosis, and thrombophlebitis. Lymphatic drainage is not advisable during acute infections, whether viral or bacterial, for heart failure, or where there is hyperthyroidism, hypertension, or malignant tumors.

TO CONCLUDE

Lymphatic drainage is a particularly delicate treatment and requires precision and gentleness. Do not be in a hurry: the treatment must last at least 15 minutes and may go on for more than an hour. You need time and a lot of practice to learn all the different movements. The minimum pressure and maximum push rule will help you avoid mistakes: if you keep to it you will not harm your patient.

ANTI-STRESS MASSAGE

The anti-stress massage differs completely from other techniques because it acts in greater depth, is more complex, and requires a greater effort on the part of the practitioner. In order to perform this technique, you must have already mastered all the techniques mentioned in the previous chapters. The anti-stress massage demands involvement, concentration, and technical skill.

TECHNIQUE

When performing anti-stress techniques, you must always observe the following fundamental rules:
- It is not enough to perform this type of massage with the palm of your hand alone, but you will have to use the whole forearm as far as the elbow.
- Constantly *rock* your partner, creating a steady, gentle swaying movement through rhythmic motions.
- Build up and maintain an atmosphere of *trust* and *confidence* with gentle but firm pressure.
- Your partner must be able to relax completely in your hands.

- *Relax* your partner through long rhythmic motions, that ebb and flow, then squeezing and draining in depth. You will see the practical application of these rules in the exercises suggested. Learn each one separately, practicing it over and over again, until you feel sufficiently confident. Then join all these movements into one massage, alternating them with long and all-embracing stroking, shaking, and rocking motions and with other movements taken from the techniques you have learned up to now.

Nearly all the mobilization exercises which I proposed at the beginning may become part of the anti-stress massage. Try introducing them during the treatment and exchange impressions with your partner as to their effectiveness. Practice will allow you to become an expert in a new, evolving, personalized massage technique. At this point you and your partner will fully share in this enriching and satisfying experience. You will have created a flow of healing and revitalizing energy which will produce the same positive effect on both of you.

1 *Begin the massage by first stroking very gently and gradually increasing your pressure. Lightly touch the legs, enveloping them with your hands and forearms.*

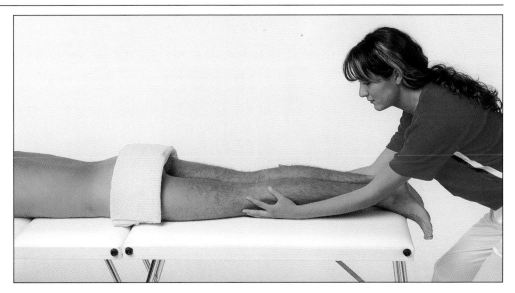

Massage toward the buttocks and with an all-involving touch work down toward the feet.

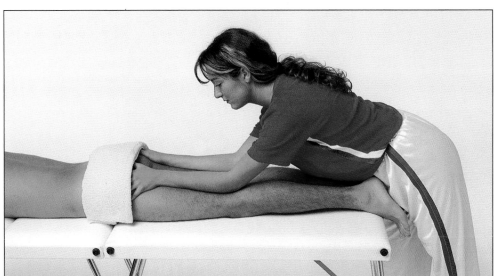

Grasp the feet and pull them gently but firmly, intermittently and rhythmically. Then let them rest. Try this technique on each leg.

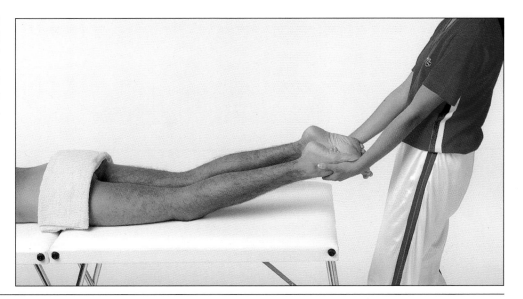

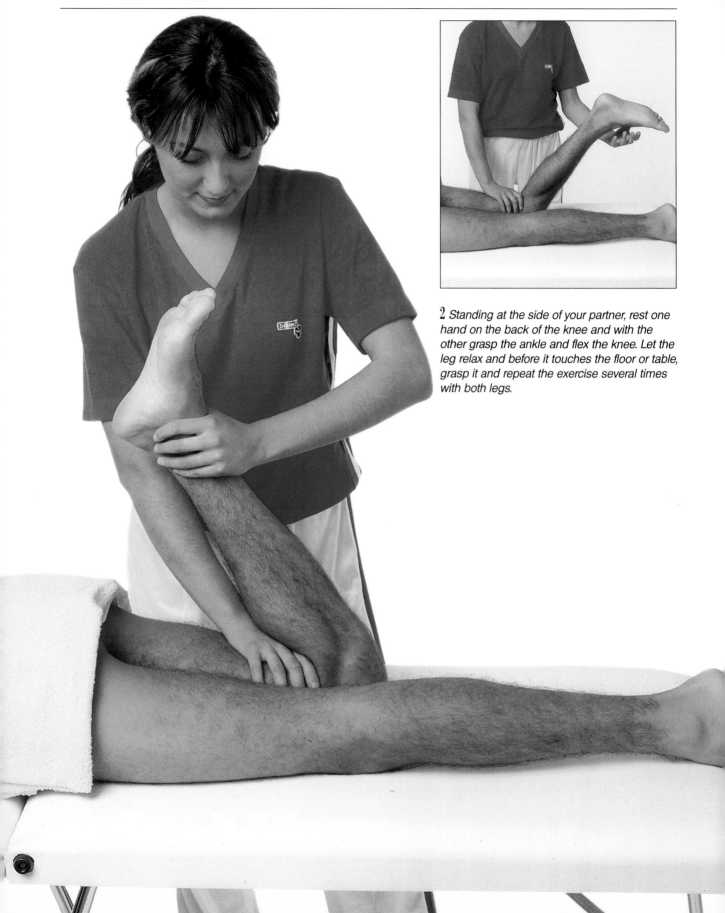

2 *Standing at the side of your partner, rest one hand on the back of the knee and with the other grasp the ankle and flex the knee. Let the leg relax and before it touches the floor or table, grasp it and repeat the exercise several times with both legs.*

3 *Stretch the muscles along one side of the body from the leg to the shoulders and back again.*

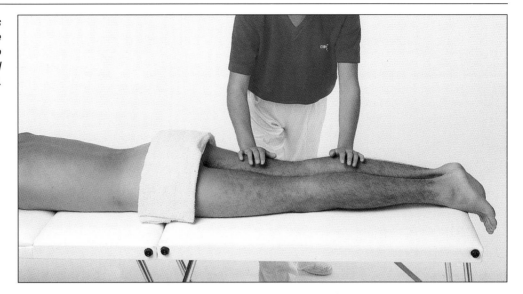

Be gentle but firm, and make sure that your partner's body is completely relaxed.

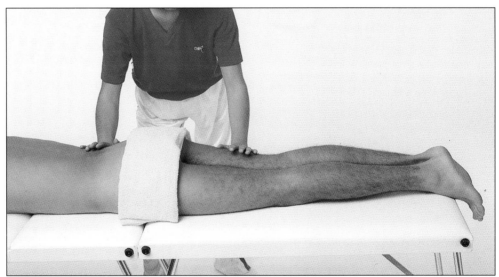

The aim of this technique is to produce a rocking motion of the body which relaxes your partner.

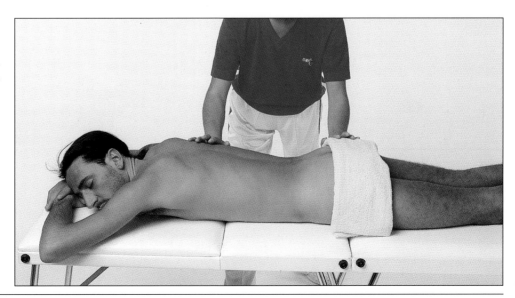

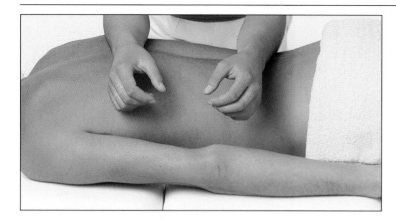

Below are a few variations you may perform during back massage:

4 Long, deep stretching performed with the forearm over the whole back.
Lengthways,

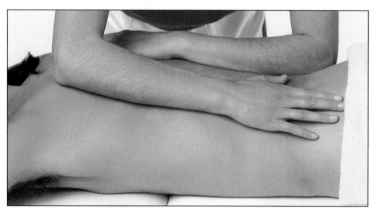

sideways,

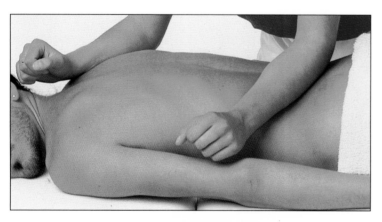

and diagonally.

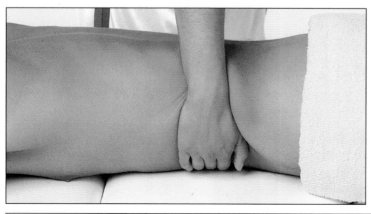

5 Rocking in ever wider movements, lift the abdomen, insert your hand flat and, without clasping with the fingers, stretch upwards and toward you, then let go.

6 *While rocking, place your hand under your partner's shoulder and stretch upwards and toward you. Let go. Repeat with the other shoulder.*

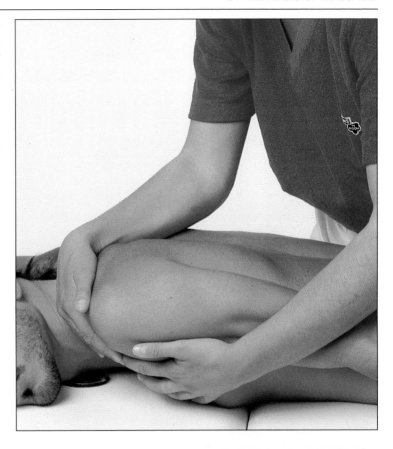

7 *Remember that these are strong movements which the partner will feel acutely. Therefore be on the alert to understand how far you can go.*

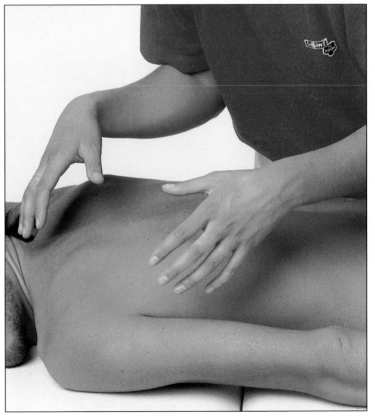

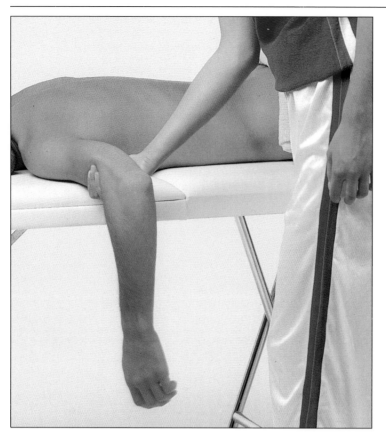

8 *Rock and shake the arm, grasping it under the elbow. Repeat with the other arm.*

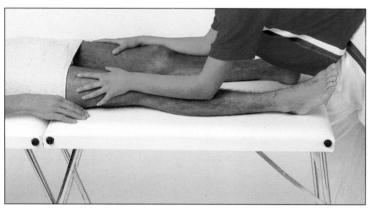

Having completed the treatment with your partner in a prone position, have him turn and begin a sustained stroking of the legs as far as the ankles and back again.

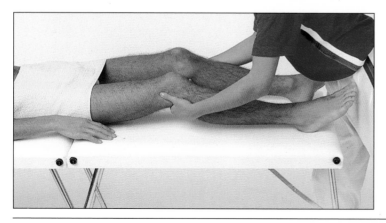

9 *During the return phase, place your hands under the partner's knees and raise them, then let them fall back. Finish the treatment by stroking as far as the feet, grasping them at the ankles and stretching them backwards rhythmically.*

10 *Use the same technique as in exercise number 5, adapting it to your partner's supine position.*

11 *Exercise 6 may also be carried out in a supine position.*

12 *Try some of the mobilization exercises which you have learned and carried out on the floor. Now use them on the table and make them part of your massage.*

13 *Try out new movements; invent, be creative, learn to communicate well-being and good energy.*

14 *When you have learned all the exercises proposed, join them into one single massage. Use and combine techniques from Swedish massage, and vary them often, experimenting with rhythm and degrees of pressure.*

SOME DON'TS

Avoid abrupt movements and sudden changes in rhythm. Always keep as much physical contact with your partner as possible. Never perform a "flat" massage, devoid of enthusiasm. You must "be there" and be aware of what you are doing.

WHEN ADVISABLE AND WHEN NOT ADVISABLE

This technique is particularly relaxing and stress-reducing, but it is also good from a hygienic point of view, as it reactivates circulation, relaxes the muscles, and helps eliminate metabolic waste. This type of massage is generally advisble, except in cases of high blood presssure, diabetes, cancer, fever, or any condition that would be compromised by such a significant increase in circulation and drainage.

TO CONCLUDE

The antistress massage is like a dance where you can enjoy the harmony created and the energy which flows. Let yourself go, be creative, try to give your patient the most pleasant experience possible, and you yourself will be amply repaid.

MASSAGE PROCEDURE

The previous pages were given over to examining the most common techniques. At this point, if you have scrupulously followed all the instructions, you should now be an experienced practitioner, able to handle most of the problems that turn up during a massage session.

Still, during this period, you have probably come up against difficulties, have had doubts and questions, and perhaps have been quite unable to solve a problem. While studying, we arrive at a point where it seems necessary to review the work done, to reconfigure all the elements of the knowledge we have gained into one complete and harmonious whole. To help you in this task, I suggest that you try the following procedure of *total massage*, one of the many types of massage possible, during which you can apply many of the techniques you have learned.

You will observe that we have not included lymph drainage and connective tissue massage as these represent in themselves a complete and highly specialized massage treatment.

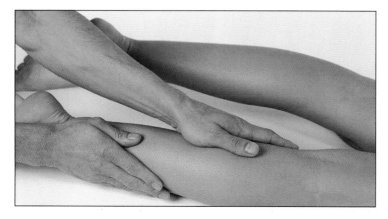

1 *With your partner lying on his stomach, start the massage by stroking the leg, beginning at the foot and going as far as the buttocks.*

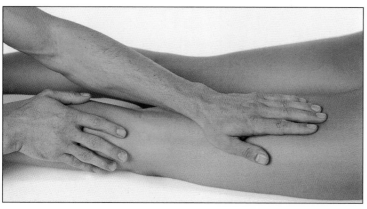

Perform long movements with a steady rhythm, gradually increasing the pressure.

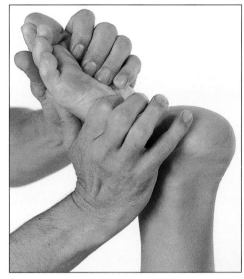

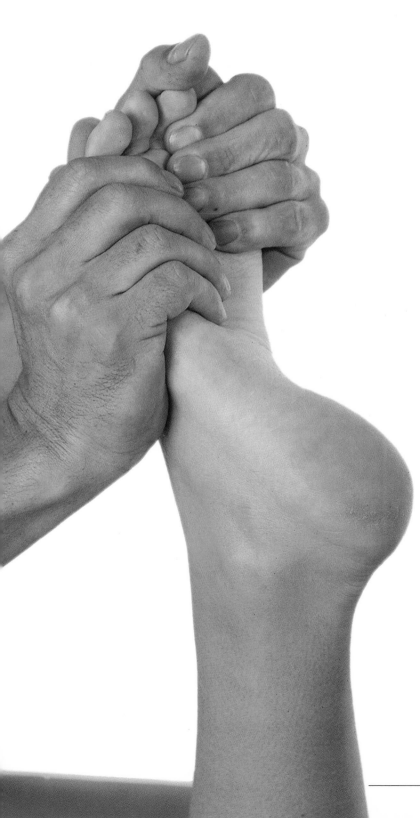

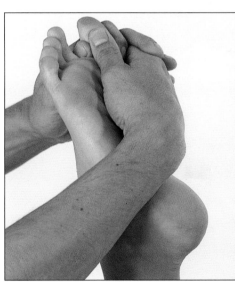

2 *Flex the leg and carry out a complete and deep massage of the foot, mobilizing the ankle, stroking, draining, and kneading with the fleshy part and the fingers.*

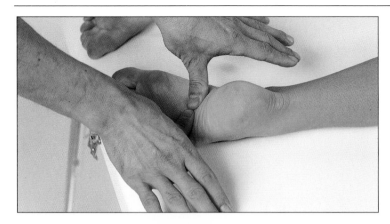

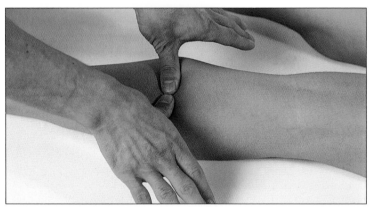

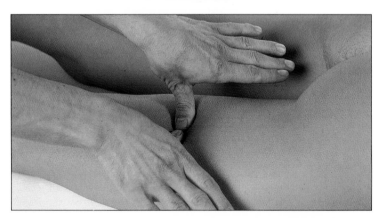

3 *With the pads of your thumbs, perform a sequence of Shiatsu movements, starting from the sole of the foot and going as far as the center of the buttock, moving about 2 cm at a time.*

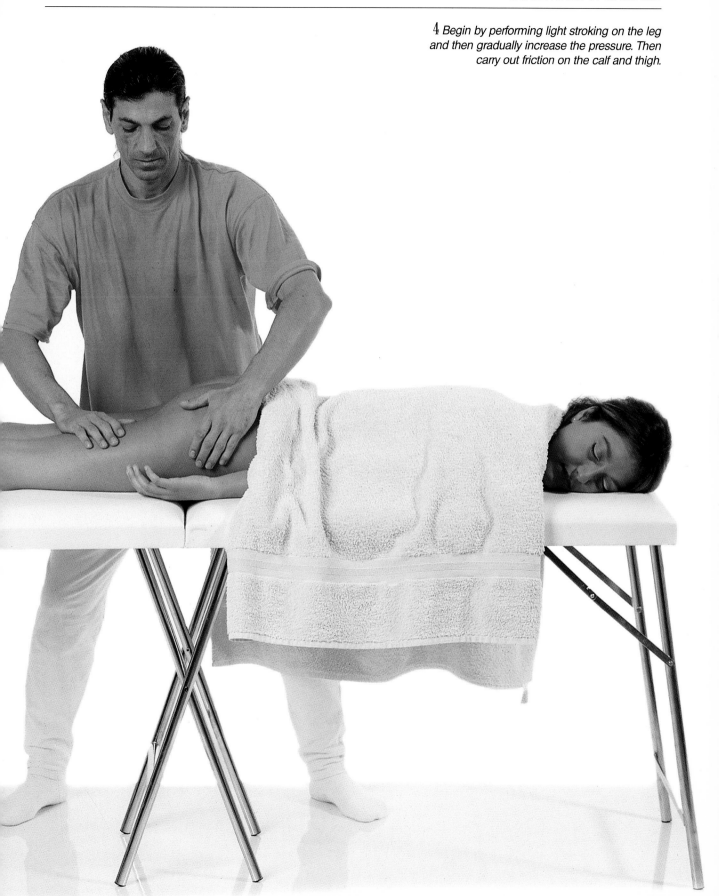

4 *Begin by performing light stroking on the leg and then gradually increase the pressure. Then carry out friction on the calf and thigh.*

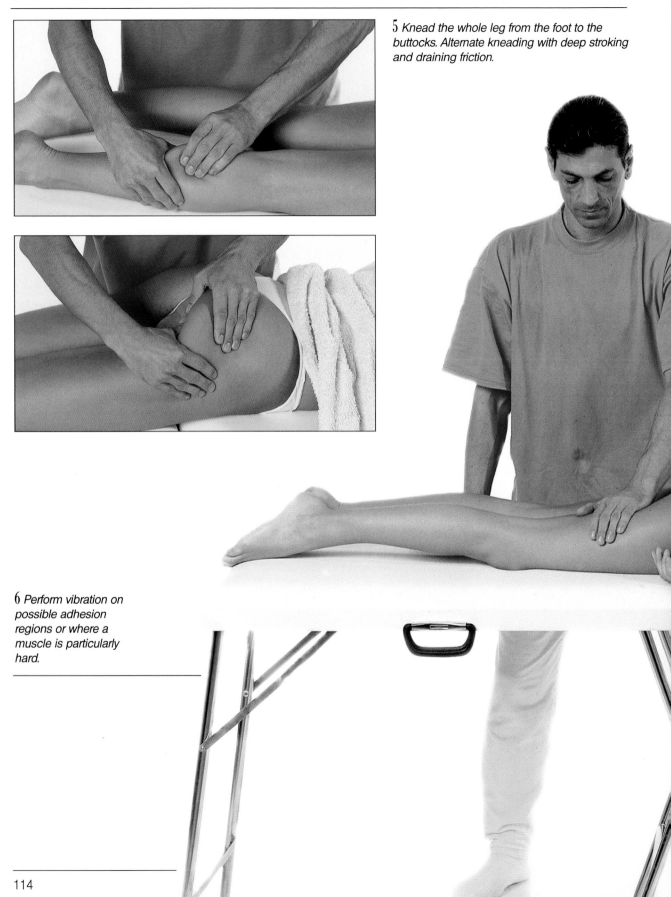

5 *Knead the whole leg from the foot to the buttocks. Alternate kneading with deep stroking and draining friction.*

6 *Perform vibration on possible adhesion regions or where a muscle is particularly hard.*

7 *Keeping your fingers flexible, you may now pass on to percussion, starting from the foot and working up to the buttocks.*

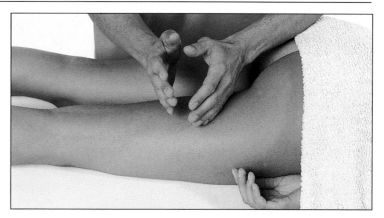

Repeat this exercise several times, always avoiding the back part of the knee.

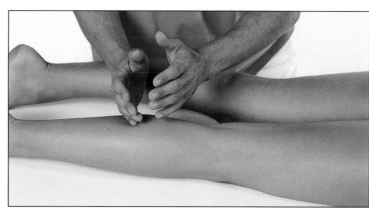

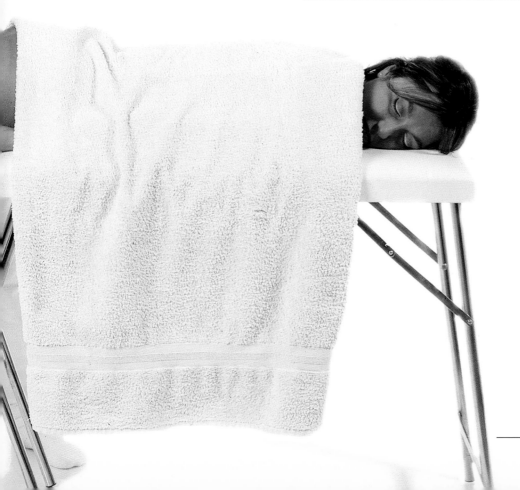

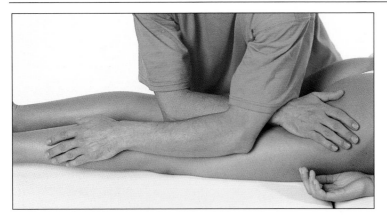

8 *Perform deep stroking and, if your partner is sufficiently relaxed, carry out more dynamic stroking.*

9 *End the leg treatment with Shiatsu, from the sole of the foot to the buttocks, moving a hand's width at a time.*

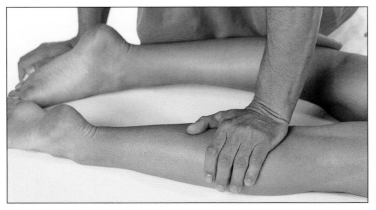

10 *Pressure exerted with the palm must be slow and deep in order to give the legs a feeling of lightness and muscle relaxation.*

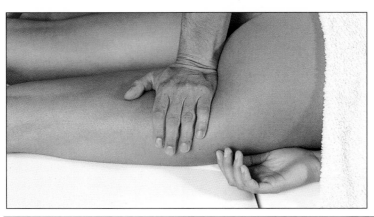

11 *Repeat the whole sequence (exercise 1 to 9) on the other leg. Then cover the legs and turn to the back. Never lose contact with your partner's body.*

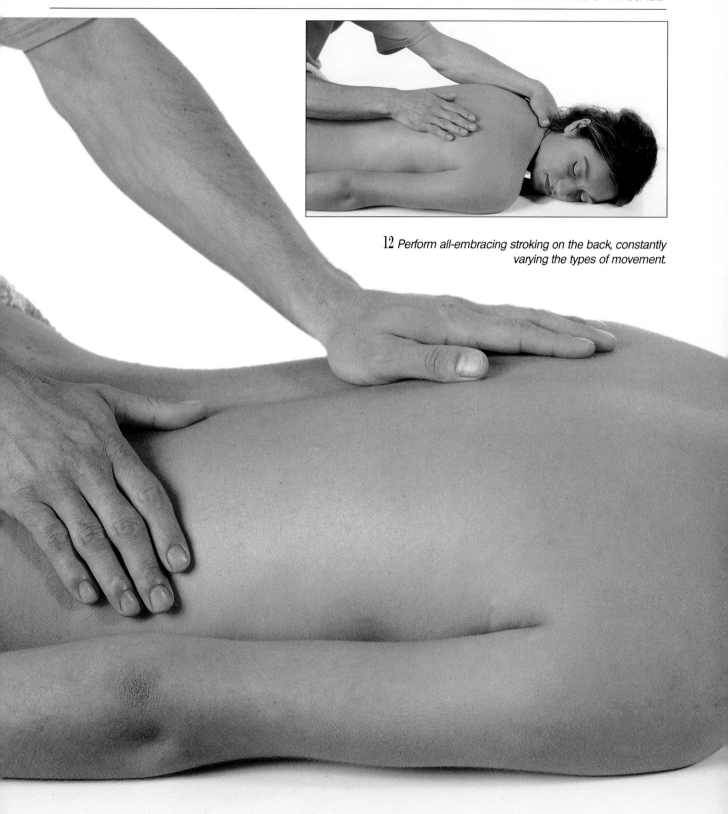

12 *Perform all-embracing stroking on the back, constantly varying the types of movement.*

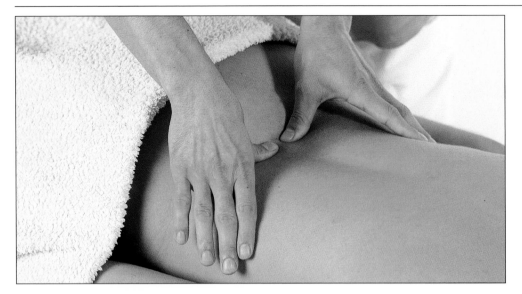

13 *Perform Shiatsu on the intravertebral spaces starting at the sacrum and moving up to the nape.*

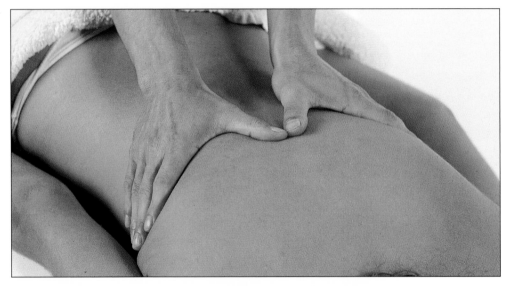

By doing this, you are treating the middle meridian which governs all the Yang meridians.

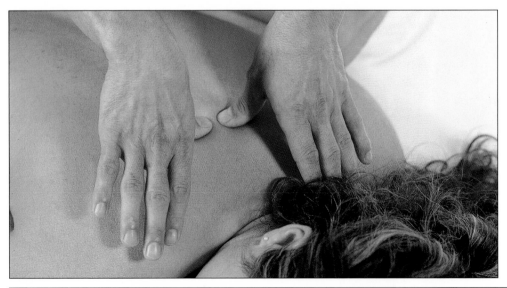

Synchronize your breathing with that of your partner. Press while exhaling and release while inhaling.

14 *Apply more light stroking, friction and finger kneading at the side of the spinal column, starting at the sacrum and moving up to the neck.*

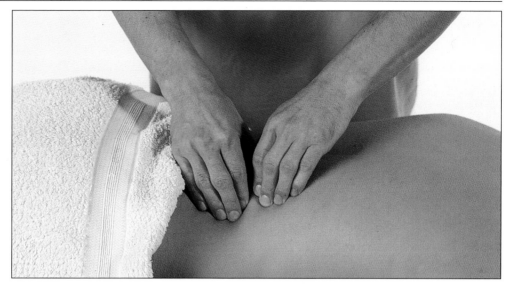

15 *First perform Shiatsu on the paravertebral muscles (bladder meridian, internal branch) and then stroke and apply finger kneading on the same area as in the previous exercise, i.e. from the sacrum to the neck.*

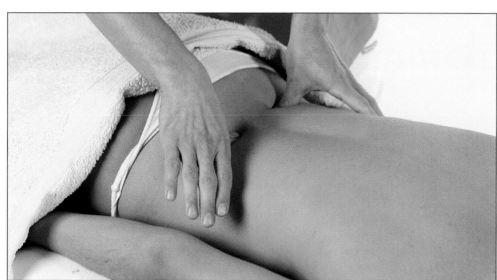

The bladder meridian situated on the back acts as a regulator of all internal organs: get used to perceiving the state of these organs through the pads of your thumbs.

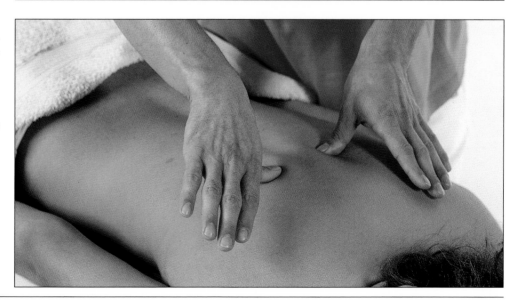

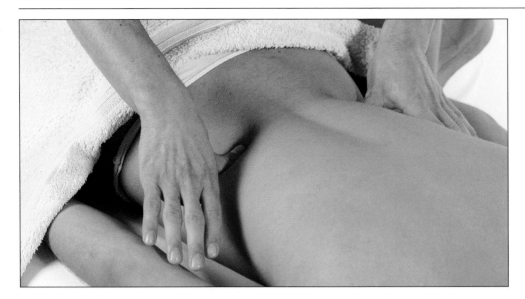

16 *Perform Shiatsu on the external branch of the bladder meridian,*

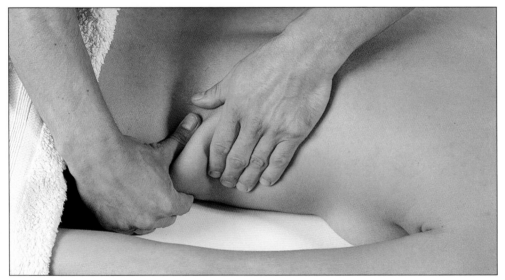

then carry out finger stroking and kneading on the same region, from the pelvis up to the shoulders.

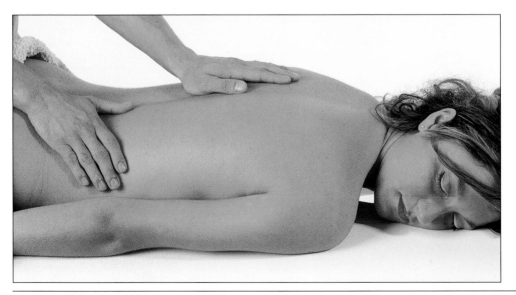

17 *Perform more stroking and friction all over the back.*

18 *Perform kneading along the whole of the back, always starting from the base of the spine and moving up to the shoulders. Knead the shoulders and the deltoids well. Alternate kneading with deep stroking and draining friction. Perform the specific variations of the kneading technique on different points of the back.*

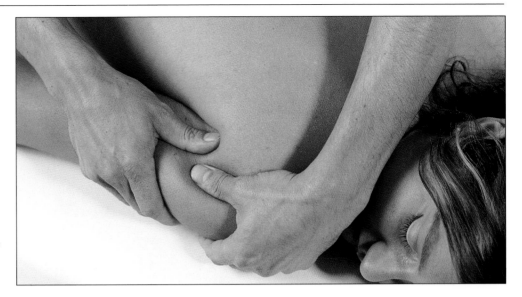

19 *Perform more stroking on the whole back, extending the movement to the arms. Friction the arms.*

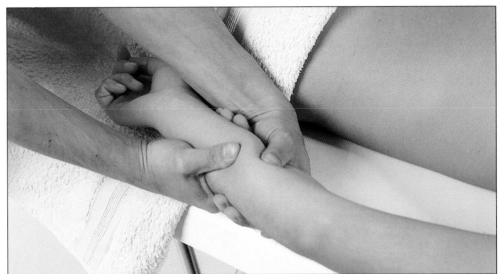

Knead your partner's hands, fingers, forearm and arm.

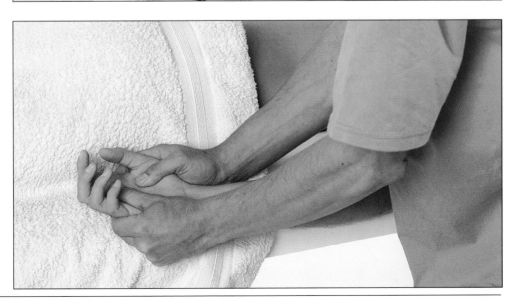

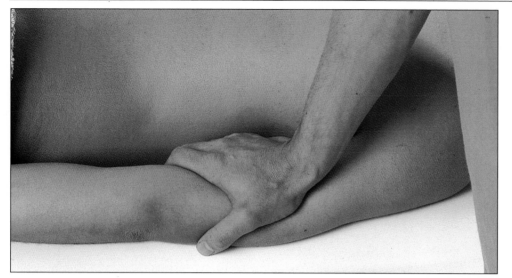

20 *Perform Shiatsu with an open palm starting at your partner's hand and going as far as the shoulder, moving a hand's width at a time.*

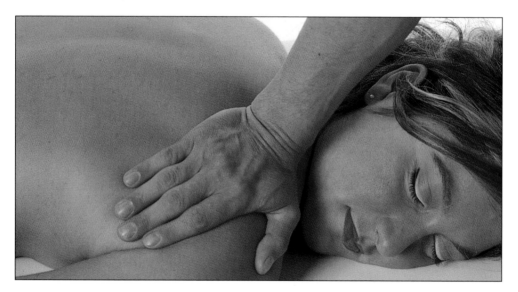

Remember that the arm is more delicate than the back, and therefore exert less pressure.

21 *Perform gentle percussion with flexible fingers. Repeat on the other arm.*

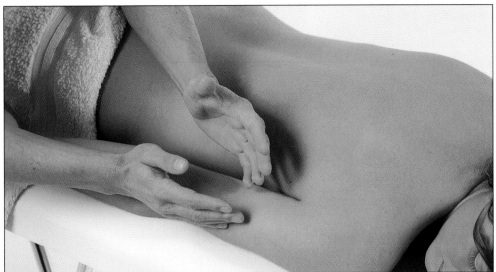

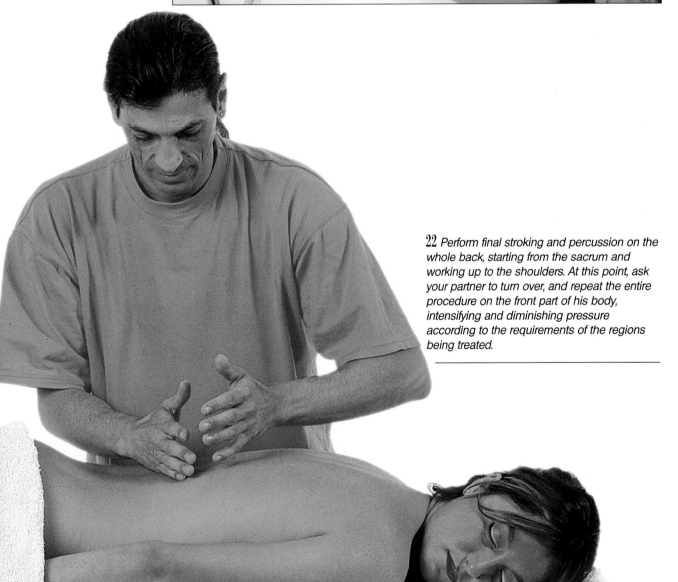

22 *Perform final stroking and percussion on the whole back, starting from the sacrum and working up to the shoulders. At this point, ask your partner to turn over, and repeat the entire procedure on the front part of his body, intensifying and diminishing pressure according to the requirements of the regions being treated.*

TO EACH HIS OWN...

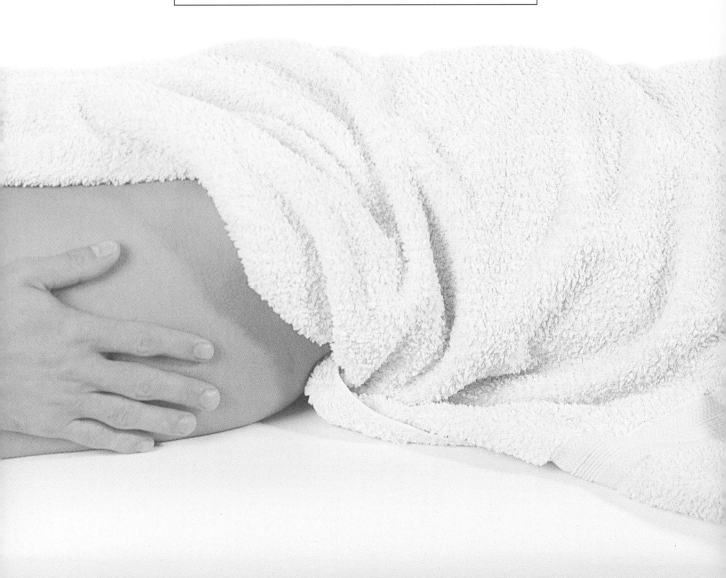

SPORTS MASSAGE

With massage for athletes, it is possible:
- to help improve the *condition* of the various organs and systems, particularly the muscular system, which are affected by sporting activities;
- to prepare for *competitive activities;*
- to help *reduce metabolic waste* from muscular activity;
- to treat the aftereffects of *sport injuries*, such as bruises, sprains and so on.
The massage you give should be appropriate to treat the demands of the particular sport, aimed, therefore, particularly at those muscle groups specifically involved. When the athlete is resuming sporting activities after a period of rest, massage must be combined with hot showers and warming up exercises gradually increasing in intensity. The idea is to bring about an increased blood flow, particularly to those muscles mostly directly involved. This is because the muscular fibers respond better to stimulation if they are at a temperature of about 39 °C. Therefore, for treatment of athletes at the beginning of their training, massage should be more energetic, decreasing in intensity as the athlete reaches greater fitness. Again, consider the nature of the specific athletic discipline in which your partner participates, in order to decide which parts of the body require particular attention.

BEFORE COMPETING

The warmup massage is gentle so as to induce relaxation if the athlete is tense and is more vigorous if there is lethargy or depression. At this point, it must be obvious that it helps to know the athlete well.
In between one competition and another, massage is very important because it relaxes the muscles and helps eliminate the waste products of metabolism which cause fatigue.
This means that massage can significantly decrease the time an athlete needs to fully recover between events.

AFTER COMPETING

The role of massage at this phase is to reduce fatigue rapidly, helping the athlete to wind down and relax, thus facilitating the avoidance of cramp. It is important to remember that some time must pass between the end of a competition and massage, so as to allow the peripheral circulation to continue its normal flow. This is also necessary in order to avoid straining the heart, which is still experiencing stress deriving from the competitive activity.

SOCCER PLAYERS

A soccer match puts an individual's stamina to the test. Soccer players often suffer from cramps and contractures, and therefore it is necessary to finish off the warming up exercises with a good stretching program. These athletes should undergo a complete Shiatsu treatment at least once a week. Particular attention should be paid to the back of the body. The massage given after the match should last longer than that given before it and should be preceded by a shower. The athlete should remain lying down, well-covered, for at least half an hour after massage.

MUSCLES AND REGIONS TO MASSAGE

All the muscles of the limbs, with particular regard to the triceps (back of the arms), the quadraceps (the front of the legs), the sacrum, the buttocks, the back extensors, and the neck muscles.

ROWERS

In rowing, the muscles of the upper part of the body are subject to a constant rhythmic and powerful effort. Massage should help maintain elasticity and balance between the upper and the lower part of the body. Massage the neck with particular care, as it is from this area that tension is discharged during the race.

MUSCLES AND AREAS TO BE MASSAGED

The neck muscles, around the scapula and arm joints, the abdominal extensors (vertebral column), quadriceps, triceps, and the calves – all these should be massaged after the shower following a race. Massage must concentrate on these same muscles, particularly on those of the back, as in the case of skiers and cyclists.

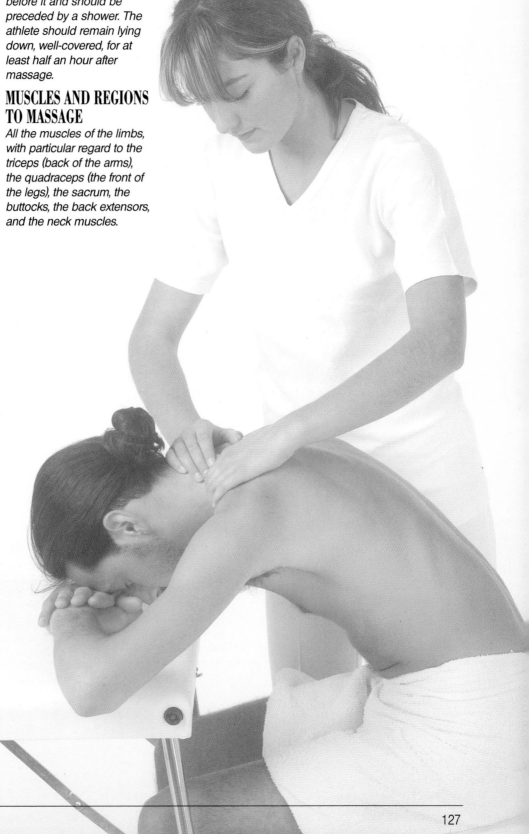

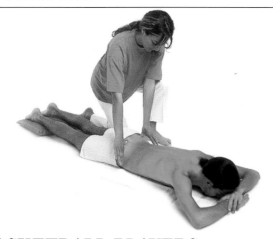

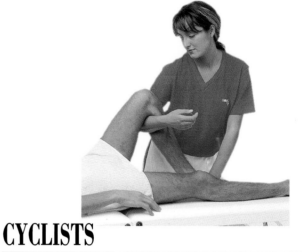

BASKETBALL PLAYERS

Massage is to be mainly concentrated on the shoulder joint, but it must be remembered that all the muscles of the back side of the body have undergone stress during the competition. Give the athlete regular Shiatsu treatments along the back side of the *body, as well as performing reflexology on the hands.*

MUSCLES AND AREAS TO BE MASSAGED

All the muscles of the body, but especially those of the forearms, the shoulders, and the calves.

CYCLISTS

During a race, these athletes assume an arched (cyphotic) position, forcing the whole back and arm muscular system into static tension. The legs, due to the prolonged effort, tend to accumulate lactic acid. Periodical Shiatsu treatments help to reduce the imbalance between the upper and lower sets of muscles.

MUSCLES AND AREAS TO BE MASSAGED

The back muscles, triceps, quadriceps, tibials and peroneals (the lower front of the leg muscles); after the race, the upper limbs and the lumbar muscles must also be treated.

BODY BUILDERS

The muscles of these athletes are extremely developed, but are short and not particularly elastic. It is important that prolonged stretching exercises complete their physical activity. Massage on body builders is tiring and often requires great arm strength. Shiatsu and reflexology provide an excellent addition to Swedish massage.

MUSCLES AND AREAS TO BE MASSAGED

All the muscles of the body.

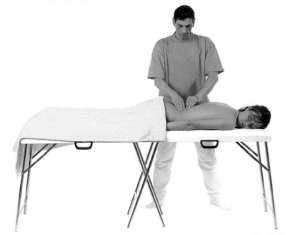

AEROBICS AND FITNESS ENTHUSIASTS

Those who practice these activities are often not professionals but amateurs wishing to keep fit or to discharge tension. The muscular effort involved produces considerable energy consumption and tonifies the athlete's cardiovascular system without, however, forming lactic acid in the muscles. All types of massage are recommended.

MUSCLES AND AREAS TO BE MASSAGED

All the muscles of the body, working, however, with greater gentleness and for longer periods than when massaging for other sports.

LONG-DISTANCE RUNNERS

Contrary to that of sprinters, the muscular effort of these athletes is extended over a prolonged period of time. It involves the white muscular fibers which are deeper and more resistant. The primary aim of the massage is to reduce the accumulation of lactic acid in the legs. Furthermore, the massage should relax the contractures which inevitably make themselves felt at the end of each athletic stint. After the race, let the athlete rest half an hour and then perform a complete massage, paying particular attention to the muscles mentioned below. For these athletes too, a weekly foot reflexology treatment can be a great help.

MUSCLES AND AREAS TO BE MASSAGED

The abdominal extensors and the buttocks require particular attention.

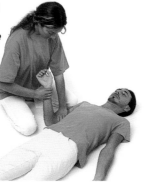

GOLFERS

Like tennis players, golfers use one part of the body more than the other and, while hitting the ball, they give a considerable twist to their body. They often complain of problems around the shoulder blades, the shoulder joints, and the elbow muscles. General equilibrium can be restored by periodical Shiatsu and hand reflexology treatments. At the end of the game, perform a long, relaxing massage, working particularly on the muscles mentioned below.

MUSCLES AND AREAS TO BE MASSAGED

The deltoid, trapezium, neck muscles, back and lumbar muscles, the buttocks, arms, and hands.

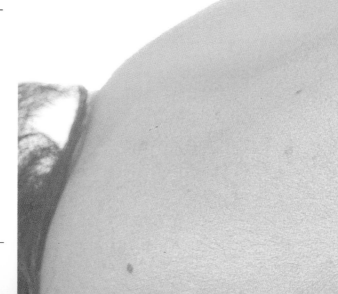

WEIGHT THROWERS

These athletes develop impressive sets of muscles in the upper part of the body through a series of exercises aimed at increasing their trophism and strength. Their muscles must be powerful and quick to be able to throw well. Massage must help keep the muscles elastic and avoid contractures and excessive shortenings.

MUSCLES AND AREAS TO BE MASSAGED

The shoulder joints and the back should be addressed. Particular treatment must also be given to the lower limbs of javelin throwers.

SWIMMERS

Swimmers are constantly massaged by water friction and develop a balanced and elastic set of muscles. Massage is not recommended for swimmers for quite some time before or after a race. Occasional Shiatsu treatments are helpful.

MUSCLES AND AREAS TO BE MASSAGED

Massage must take into account the whole body and should not be applied too vigorously so that it doesn't interfere with the gentle and rhythmic movements typical of swimming.

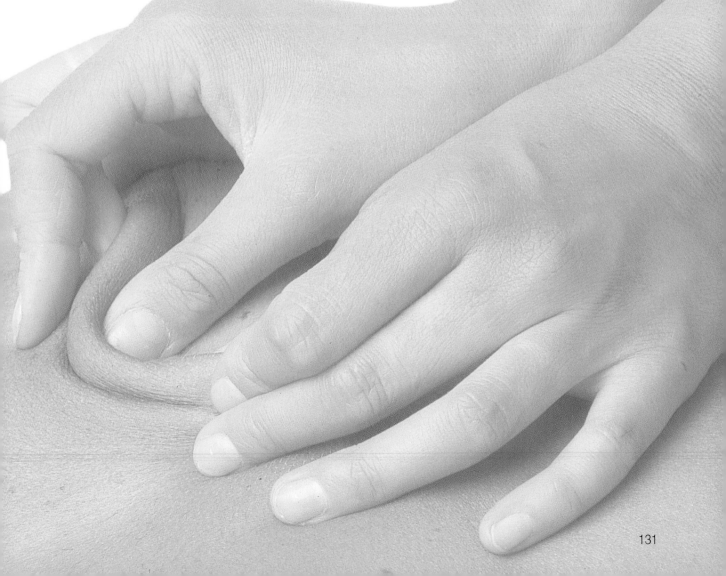

BOXERS

Strength and agility are of the essence for these athletes, who must also possess a considerable force of resistance. During their athletic preparation, alternate muscle training with Shiatsu. Work up the elasticity of the shoulders and the leg muscles.

MUSCLES AND AREAS TO BE MASSAGED

The forearms, arms, deltoids, shoulder joints, vertebral column extensors, abdominal muscles, triceps, and Achilles tendon.

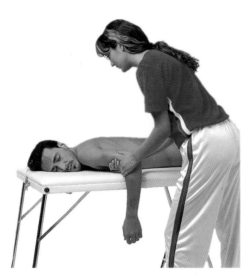

HIGH JUMPERS, LONG JUMPERS

These jumpers have strong, springy muscles. Before a race, warm up the calves and the thigh muscles. End off with a well-balanced treatment of all the muscles mentioned below.

MUSCLES AND AREAS TO BE MASSAGED

Massage the achilles tendon, triceps, quadriceps, buttocks, and, to a lesser degree, the back muscles. Add a foot reflexology treatment, together with mobilization of the foot joints to finish off.

WEIGHT LIFTERS

Due to the great mass and high tone of this type of athlete's muscles, this person is difficult to massage. Improve his muscular elasticity by stretching and Shiatsu.

MUSCLES AND AREAS TO BE MASSAGED

All the muscles of the body, with particular regard to the arms, the forearms, the shoulders, and the back.

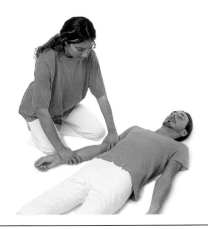

SKIERS

Emphasis must be put on either agility or resistance according to the speciality in which these athletes are engaged. Care must be devoted to the legs, activating also all the joints from the hip to the foot.

MUSCLES AND AREAS TO BE MASSAGED

After the warm up, massage the whole body paying particular attention to the calves, the back, the forearms, and the shoulders. After the competition, concentrate also on the hands and the upper limbs, particularly for cross-country skiers who make considerable use of ski poles.

TENNIS PLAYERS

These athletes mainly use one arm, therefore it is necessary that they undergo an intense series of exercises aimed at re-establishing a proper equilibrium. Frequent Shiatsu and hand reflexology treatments contribute to maintaining this balance. After the match and a long, warm shower, carry out an overall massage, and let the athlete rest stretched out on the table or floor.

MUSCLES AND AREAS TO BE MASSAGED

Massage not only the muscles of the back, the shoulder and the arm, but also the abdominal muscles, quadriceps, and calves.

SPRINTERS

The intense performance of the athletes engaged in this discipline is realized in a matter of seconds and burns up a massive dose of oxygen. Before the race, warm up the leg muscles with a short but tonifying massage. Then, wait a moment until all the physiological functions have returned to their normal level. Then eliminate the remaining tensions, massaging all the below-mentioned muscles. A weekly treatment of foot reflexology helps sprinters to keep their feet healthy and fit.

MUSCLES AND AREAS TO BE MASSAGED

The soles of the feet, the toes, the Achilles tendon, triceps, sacrum, and the vertebral column extensors. Do not forget to concentrate also, even if to a lesser degree, on the deltoids.

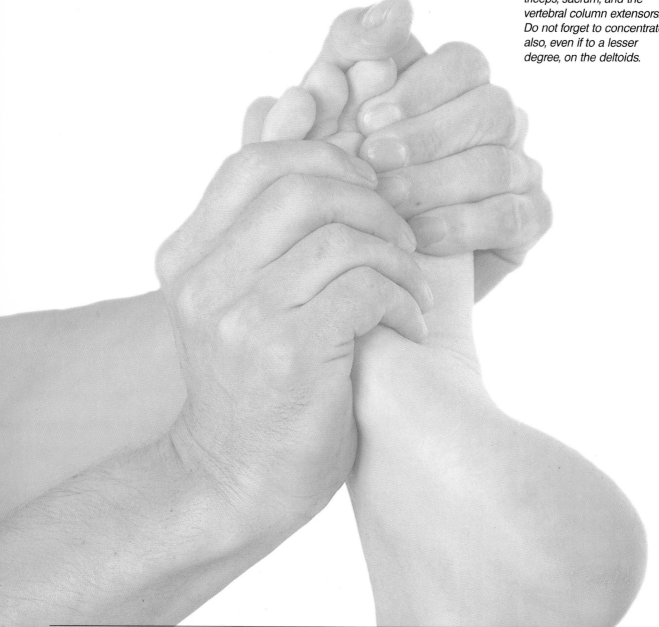

SPECIAL CATEGORY MASSAGE

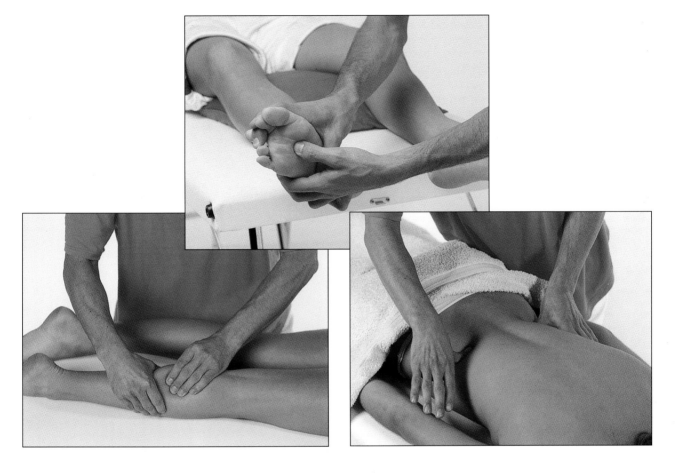

Whenever you work with new people doing massage, always find out details about any problems they may have; ask about the duration and frequency of any disorders they experience; enquire about their type of work and whether it aggravates their symptoms; seek information on their diet and sleeping habits, and try to understand if they suffer from stress or anxiety. Finally, don't forget that each patient is unique, with a special personal history, psychology, and particular physical characteristics.

Therefore, do not make the mistake of hastily classifying anyone in one of the categories I have suggested, because you run the risk of neglecting important information which could be essential for adapting a plan of treatment to that person's specific case.

To simplify matters for those of you who are novices and to provide some useful information, I have thought it advisable to group together into "Special Categories" those cases you are likely to meet. In these categories will be found almost all types of massage, with the exception of curative massage for specific problems. Each category presents characteristics common to all, which mostly derive from particular postures held over long periods. The information you receive from your partner will help to tell you what category of massage is appropriate and to plan a suitable treatment program.

THE ELDERLY

People of a certain age suffer from a series of infirmities due to the wear and tear on joints, to osteoporosis, and to previous injuries which, all adding up together over the years, leave painful effects which often become acute in moments of tiredness or when the weather changes. If there are no specific illnesses and if the doctor does not advise against it, Swedish massage or foot reflexology can be of great benefit. Remember, however, that the body of an elderly person is more sensitive and delicate than that of a younger person. Massage should therefore be gentle and slow, keeping stimulation to a minimum. At the end of the massage, allow your partner to lie resting for some moments. Assist that person in getting up in case a sudden drop in blood pressure should cause instability.

CHILDREN

Children rarely need massage for stress or physical problems. More often physical contact for them is a means to communicate feelings and emotions which they cannot otherwise express in words. Massaging my children is for me and for them an incomparable moment of play and communication. They decide how, when and where they are to be massaged, and this gives me the chance to cuddle and caress them just as much as they unconsciously need. For children, massage is a way to discover their bodies, to develop their awareness of themselves, and to become conscious of their identity. I advise both mothers and especially fathers to massage their children. Do not bother about particular techniques; be guided by your instinct and your heart, and you can be sure you will never go wrong.

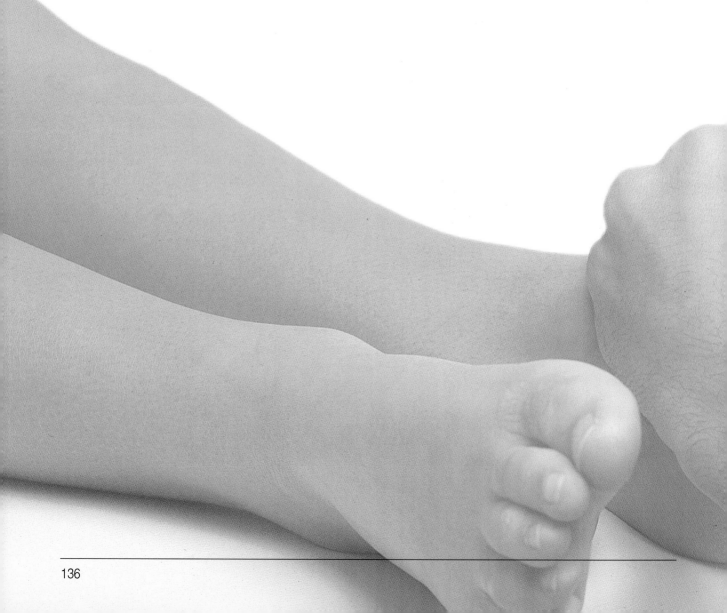

TRUCK DRIVERS

Truck drivers and all those who pass many hours at the steering wheel (delivery men, taxi drivers, chauffeurs, commercial travellers) often suffer from lumbar trouble, sometimes accompanied by sciatica type pain. In these cases, a series of gymnastic exercises concentrated on posture errors can be useful in re-establishing the balance in the pelvis. Add to these a dozen or so massages on the lumbar region, as advised for trades people. If the person complains of frequent tiredness, periodic Shiatsu treatments are advised, particularly along the back of the body. Face massage also helps eliminate tiredness and the wrinkles on the face deriving from tension while driving.

SERVICE PEOPLE

In this category are numbered all those who stand while working, such as bartenders, shop assistants, restaurant owners, and in general all those who work behind a counter dealing with the public. Besides psychological tension, people of this category almost always suffer from circulation problems in the lower limbs, swollen ankles, edema, painful hip and knee joints, sore feet, and lumbago. Manual lymphatic drainage on the legs, alternated with Shiatsu carried out with the palm of the hands, helps to solve circulation problems, while foot reflexology gives relief to tired feet. Lumbago can be relieved by massaging the back and the buttocks, after placing a cushion under the abdomen to flex the lumbar vertebrae.

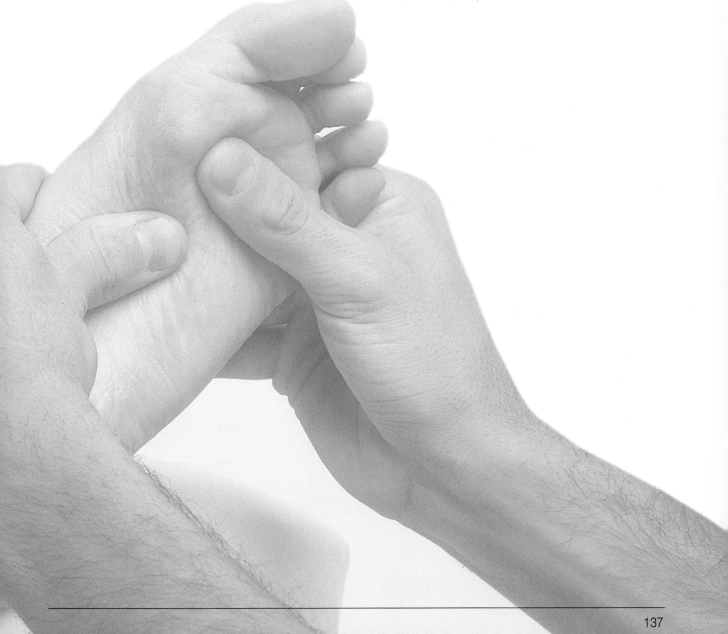

OFFICE WORKERS

In this category are numbered all those who constantly work behind a desk, teachers, designers, and students included. People in this category often freeze into one typical posture, with a curved back and hunched shoulders: all the tension tends to be held in the neck muscles and particularly on to the

trapezius. Such people often suffer from headaches and eye tensions. Furthermore, their activity is more mental than physical. A long massage on the face and skull carried out in a congenial environment, and with relaxing music playing softly in the background, works wonders on these people. Also a foot bath with very hot water and bath salts, followed by a foot reflexology treatment is very beneficial. Periodical Shiatsu treatments on the whole body help dispel tension.

AESTHETIC MASSAGE

Ninety-nine percent of women swear they have more or less serious aesthetic problems such as being overweight, cellulitis, stretch marks; fat deposits on the thighs, on the buttocks, on the abdomen; wrinkles on their face, fragile veins, swelling, and water retention in the legs. Massage alone is practically never enough to solve these problems. For the body to be beautiful, it has to be healthy, and it would therefore be appropriate to begin a discussion with people who have these concerns about the importance of a balanced diet, of regular exercise in a specific activity, of cutting down smoking, of drinking lots of water, and of looking after their bodies with great love and care.

Stress too plays a part in bringing about these problems; therefore it would be advisable to suggest that they frequent either relaxation or yoga classes and combine these with antistress massage. With regards to massage for purely aesthetic reasons, that is massage against cellulitus, there are so many different methods and as many variations: lymph drainage for circulation problems; Swedish massage, particularly kneading and deep drainages for fat deposits; gentle and stroking massage with oil essences to limit aesthetic damage caused by stretch marks. And again, use face massage to attenuate wrinkles.

POST-PREGNANCY

For many reasons, this category is very much a category on its own. To begin with, new mothers are often depressed and stressed because of childbirth and the new situation in which they find themselves: a weekly antistress massage will help them regain their good humor and give them the strength to face their day more serenely. The physiological changes which occur during pregnancy practically always bring about a series of aesthetic changes (cellulitus, relaxation of the muscles, circulation problems) which may be solved by following a combined diet, gymnastic, and massage program. Lymphatic drainage and Swedish massage are advisable in these cases. Due to the alterations in the body's physiological balances, women who have recently given birth often also suffer from small aches and pains such as discomfort in the lumbar region, a stiff neck and sore shoulders, and heaviness in the legs. Shiatsu and foot reflexology restore the lost balance and are a great help in solving the greater part of these problems. Practically all types of massage are beneficial to this category. Remember, however, that during the first forty days after childbirth, nature follows its natural course in restoring the body's equilibrium. Therefore during this period you must be very careful and perform light, gentle, short massages.

THE STRESSED

We all suffer, in different degrees, from some sort of stress, and we all tend to somatize as aches and pains the psychic and emotive tensions we are forced to endure at work and in our lives in general. There are people who are more sensitive and reactive than others, who react so badly to the daily hurdles with which they are confronted that they either fall into a deep depression or become excessively anxious. A defense mechanism is then created, a barrier against the outside world which means to protect them but instead merely gives rise to muscular tension, stiffness, and a dimming of the senses.
Such people have a real need to rediscover their own body and to regain gently their ability to feel and to perceive their muscles and skin. An antistress massage, if carried out by expert hands, can work wonders because it helps those who are stressed to recapture their sense of well-being and joy of life. This awareness of one's own body helps eliminate tensions and fears. Foot reflexology and Shiatsu also can play an important role in bringing people who are overly stressed back to a sense of normality. These techniques, however, must be used with great prudence and sensitivity so as to avoid causing excessive responses which are contrary to those intended.

MASSAGE AND AROMATHERAPY

At the beginning of this manual, I spoke of products that one can use during a massage.
The practitioner has complete liberty to choose them. The oil or other products serve only to limit the friction between your hands and your partner's body. There is, however, a particular category of oils, essential oils, with unique characteristics that make them a treatment unto themselves.

ADVICE FOR USE

An essential oil is a product obtained by pressing, crushing, or distilling the leaves, flowers, or fruits of different plants. Essences are volatile and photosensitive, and must therefore be preserved hermetically sealed in a dark, airy place in containers of dark glass or metal. An essential oil must not be used in its pure state for a massage, but diluted in pure vegetable oil of a good, delicate quality. The oil derived from avocado, hazel nut, wheat germ, grapeseed, or sweet almond are excellent in this regard. When an essential oil is diluted, it becomes rancid more quickly, therefore take care to mix only the quantity to be used within a month or so. Wheat germ oil is antioxidant and increases the life span of the product. As an alternative, you could pour a spoonful of diluting oil into a small container and then add the drops of essence oil. Use the entire contents during the massage. It is very important that the proportions of essence and diluting oils be correct. A basic rule is that the higher the toxicity, the weaker the concentration. Another rule is that for physical problems, the concentration should be higher than that used for problems of a more psychological and emotional nature. These are merely general rules to which you will have to apply your own personal experience, testing, and retesting, and learning from your own mistakes. In the beginning keep to the prescribed doses or even less, and increase the concentration only if you do not achieve the desired results.

ESSENCES TO BE USED

Essences may be divided or subdivided into three groups:
- *high tone* oils, stimulating and energy giving;
- *medium tone* oils, mostly used to treat physical disorders;
- *basic tone* oils, calming and sedating.
This general subdivision should give you an idea of the group from which to choose an essence or essences for a given treatment. Use one to four oils to create the mixture, never more than this, and to make your choice, follow this method. Establish which is the main disorder to be treated and check from the following list which oils suit your case. If there are also secondary disorders, repeat the above operation and check which oils are suitable for the main disorder and which are also usable for the secondary one. If after this selection, the list of oils exceeds four, choose one to four out of these, and pour two drops of each in a small container, adding also a teaspoon of basic oil. If the perfume is agreable both to you and to your patient, then that is the right mixture.
As a help, I will indicate which essences mix well together and suggest some prescriptions for everyday problems. The quantities shown indicate the maximum number of drops to be used of each essence. You will have no difficulty reducing the proportions in order to obtain a less concentrated mixture.

THERAPEUTIC PROPERTIES

ANALGESIC: *geranium, ginger, lavender, oregano, rosemary, sage*
ANTIARTHRITIS: *cypress, lemon, juniper, thyme*
ANTICELLULITIS: *cypress, fennel, lavender, lemon, rosemary, sage*
ANTI-INFLAMMATORY: *calendula*
ANTIRHEUMATIC: *cypress, eucalyptus, hyssop, juniper, lavender, thyme*
ANTISTRESS: *fennel, hyssop, lemon, orange, rose, sandalwood*
ANTISTRETCH MARKS: *chamomille, jasmine, yarrow*
ASTRINGENT: *cypress, geranium, lemon, juniper, mint, rosemary*
CALMING: *cypress, geranium, lavender, sage, sandalwood*
CIRCULATION STIMULANTS: *geranium, lavender, rosemary, sage*
DECONGESTANTS: *eucalyptus, lavender, mint, pine, rosemary*
DECONGESTANTS AND DIURETICS: *camphor, cypress, fennel, hyssop, rosemary, sage, sandalwood*
MUSCULAR RELAXATION: *basil, cypress, oregano, rosemary, thyme*
PAIN KILLERS *(muscular pains): eucalyptus, ginger, juniper, lavender, marjoram, pine, rosemary, ylang ylang*
FOOT STIMULANTS: *rose, rosemary, sandalwood*
TONERS: *citronella, lavender, lemon, rosemary*

PRESCRIPTIONS

ARTHRITIS: *6 chamomille, 8 rosemary, 8 sage*
BRONCHITIS: *15 eucalyptus, 10 hyssop, 5 sandalwood*
CELLULITIS: *12 fennel, 4 juniper, 8 rosemary, 8 sage*
CHILBLAINS: 15 lemon, 15 marigold
CIRCULATION STIMULANTS: *4 cinnamon, 12 juniper, 8 rosemary*
CRAMPS: *15 basil, 15 oregano*
DERMATITIS: *6 bergamot, 12 geranium, 6 juniper, 6 lavender*
INSOMNIA: *4 chamomille, 4 juniper, 6 orange*
MIGRAINE: *5 lavender, 10 lemon balm, 5 oregano, 10 sage*
MUSCLE TONER: *8 cinnamon, 8 citronella, 8 lavender*
MYALGIA: *8 eucalyptus, 8 rosemary, 12 sage*
NERVOUS TENSION: *3 basil, 3 juniper, 3 lavender, 3 ylang ylang*
SINUSITIS: *8 basil, 8 eucalyptus, 8 lavender, 8 peppermint*

Now try to create your own mixtures basing your experiments on the indications given for each oil, on the simple rules described above, and on your own intuition.

WARNING

- Keep the oils out of the reach of children.
- Never swallow the oils in their pure state.
- Keep from contact with eyes.
- Always dilute before use.
- Avoid exposing the oils to the sun.
- Keep the oils hermetically sealed in a dark place.

BERGAMOT

This fruit is cultivated particularly in Italy and the oil is derived from pressing its skin.

HIGH TONE OIL:
it has a fresh fragrance, similar to that of the lemon and is used in many perfumes.

THERAPEUTIC PROPERTIES:
it is strongly antiseptic and effective against infections in any part of the body. It is indicated in cases of colic, gastroenteritis, bladder and urinary infections, acne, herpes, ulcers, psoriasis, tonsilitis, and bronchitis. As it is a high tone oil, it is useful against anxiety and depression. It has anti-tumor properties, both as a preventive measure and as treatment.

WARNING:
bergamot may cause pigmentation of the skin. It must not therefore be used in the pure state on the skin and never before exposure to the sun.

IT MIXES WELL WITH:
cypress, jasmine, lavender, and lemon.

FOR MASSAGE:
use it on the face for acne, and on the scalp.

CINNAMON

This is a spice from the East, and the oil is distilled from its leaves and bark.

BASIC TONE OIL:
it has a warm, spicy perfume.

THERAPEUTIC PROPERTIES:
digestive and antiseptic, it helps fight the common cold, produces heat, and is a good general stimulant. It is effective against mycosis (fungal disease) and candida.

WARNING:
if not sufficiently diluted, it can cause irritation.

IT MIXES WELL WITH:
rosemary, sandalwood, and cypress.

FOR MASSAGE:
as it is a stimulant and produces heat, it is excellent as a precompetition massage oil.

CLOVE

This spice originates from Asia. The oil is obtained by distilling the clove whose bud has not yet opened.

MEDIUM TONE OIL:
it has a strong, sweet perfume.

THERAPEUTIC PROPERTIES:
it is a powerful antiseptic against infections of the digestive tract. It is an analgesic and a lenitive; it calms itchiness, improves breathing, and helps sleep.

WARNING:
use it well diluted to avoid irritation.

IT MIXES WELL WITH:
cinnamon, frankincense, and rosemary.

FOR MASSAGE:
it is excellent for curative massage, in solving problems deriving from sprains and the overstretching of the muscles.

CYPRESS

This essence is obtained by distilling the flowers, the leaves, and the branches of the plant.

MEDIUM TONE OIL:
spicy, balsamic, and refreshing.

THERAPEUTIC PROPERTIES:
it has antispasm properties and is indicated for problems relating to the air passages. It has an astringent effect and is therefore indicated also for hemorrhages, menstrual periods, varicose veins, and slow circulation.

WARNING:
if you prepare a bottle of massage oil which contains cypress, remember to use it within two or three months of the date of preparation.

IT MIXES WELL WITH:
lemon, orange, and rose.

FOR MASSAGE:
include this essence in the preparation of oils for massage to reduce cellulitis or to treat cramps and muscular stiffness.

EUCALYPTUS

This essence is made from the fresh leaves of the tree, which originates from Australia.

SUPERIOR TONE OIL:
it has a woody, sweet fragrance, similar to that of camphor.

THERAPEUTIC PROPERTIES:
it is mainly used against infections of the respiratory tract such as bronchitis or sinusitis, as it facilitates breathing. It is excellent at reducing fever; it has anti-inflammatory properties; it helps in cases of bladder infections, herpes, ulcers, catarrh, and diarrhea. It also possesses diuretic properties.

WARNING:
dilute it, as it can cause irritation of the skin.

IT MIXES WELL WITH:
marjoram, lavender, and pine.

FOR MASSAGE:
a gentle massage with this oil around the shoulders and the chest helps decongest the airways in case of infection.

FRANKINCENSE

It grows in Arab countries. It is distilled from the resin which oozes from its bark.

BASIC TONE OIL:
its fragrance induces relaxation and meditation.

THERAPEUTIC PROPERTIES:
it helps breathing and is astringent, tonifying, and antiseptic.

WARNING:
frankincense is suitable for external use only.

IT MIXES WELL WITH:
juniper, cloves, and sandalwood.

FOR MASSAGE:
thanks to its toning and astringent properties, it is an excellent oil for aesthetic massage.

JASMINE

It originates from the Far East and is cultivated in the Mediterranean. Jasmine essence is the most expensive oil, but small concentrations are enough to achieve the desired results.

BASIC TONE OIL:
it has a very intense fragrance, similar to that of the rose.

THERAPEUTIC PROPERTIES:
it regulates menstruation and fights frigidity (it is considered an aphrodisiac),
headaches, and cramps. It is useful for problems of a psychological nature, as it has a calming and relaxing effect.

WARNING:
jasmine is suitable for external use only.

IT MIXES WELL WITH:
all oils, but especially those derived from citrus fruits.

FOR MASSAGE:
it is ideal for all types of massage, but particularly for a complete antistress massage.

JUNIPER

Juniper oil is distilled from the dry fruits of the Juniper tree. It grows in Europe and Canada.

MEDIUM TONE OIL:
it is used to give an aroma to gin. With time and with exposure to air and light, it becomes darker and thicker.

THERAPEUTICAL PROPERTIES:
it is antiseptic,
diuretic, and helps fight anxiety states. Though stimulating to the circulatory system, it calms rheumatic and menstrual pains. Also a nervous system toner, juniper fights anxiety, stress and insomnia. It is useful against acne, eczema, and seborrhea.

WARNING:
juniper should not be
used during pregnancy.

IT MIXES WELL WITH:
cypress, frankincense, lavender, and sandalwood.

FOR MASSAGE:
excellent for use after prolonged physical exercise, juniper helps to reduce muscular pain and fatigue.

LAVENDER

It is one of the most widely used oils, thanks to its versatility. The essence is distilled from its oil-rich flowers, leaves, and stalks.

MEDIUM OIL TONE:
its well-known fragrance dissipates quickly.

THERAPEUTIC PROPERTIES:
particularly if used in combination with other oils, lavender is effective in treating problems that have to do with nerves. It fights high blood pressure, lymphatic congestion, flatulence, nausea, gastroenteritis, bladder infections, dysmenorrhea, muscular pains, rheumatisms and sprains, anxiety, depression, cellulitis, and water retention.

WARNING:
lavender is one of the oils most subjected to adulterations, therefore be sure to buy a good oil for your treatments.

IT MIXES WELL WITH:
most oils, particularly with orange, pine, and rosemary.

FOR MASSAGE:
use it for lymphatic drainage and aesthetic treatments aimed at reducing cellulite.

LEMON BALM

This plant grows spontaneously in Italy, and the oil is distilled from its leaves and flowers.

BASIC OIL TONE:
its fragrance is similar to that of lemon.

THERAPEUTIC PROPERTIES:
it has a soothing effect on insect bites and is useful against anxiety, insomnia, and headaches.

WARNING:
it is an absolutely innocuous plant, but its oil must not be used in its pure state.

IT MIXES WELL WITH:
lavender, lemon, and rosemary.

FOR MASSAGE:
use it combined with rosemary to soothe muscular pain and rheumatism.

MARJORAM

Belonging to the mint family, Marjoram has a pungent perfume. Legend has it that it was Aphrodite, the Greek goddess of love, who created it as the symbol of happiness.

BASIC TONE OIL:
its fragrance is pungent and intense.

THERAPEUTIC PROPERTIES:
antiseptic and antispasmodic, marjoram is also sedative and acts against insomnia and stress. It is useful against contractures, rheumatism, bronchitis, sinusitis and menstrual pains.

WARNING:
avoid taking during pregnancy. Do not exceed doses so as to avoid excessive relaxation.

IT MIXES WELL WITH:
eucalyptus, lavender, and rosemary.

FOR MASSAGE:
this oil is excellent for use after intense physical exercise. Use it together with eucalyptus and rosemary to massage tired and contracted muscles following a race, then allow the athlete to rest on the table floor for at least half an hour, wrapped in a warm blanket.

NUTMEG

It grows particularly in India. This oil is extracted through vapor distillation.

MEDIUM OIL TONE:
it has a very pungent and intense aroma.

THERAPEUTIC PROPERTIES:
nutmeg helps digestion and fights intestinal infections. Although it is, in fact, a stimulant, it is also effective against toothaches, muscle pain, and fatigue.

WARNING:
do not exceed prescribed doses. Nutmeg can be toxic.

IT MIXES WELL WITH:
marjoram and rosemary.

FOR MASSAGE:
thanks to its analgesic properties, it is excellent for back massage (arthrosis) and for massage on the leg muscles following a race.

ORANGE

This oil is distilled from bitter orange flowers. It is precious, very expensive, and of superior quality.

BASIC TONE OIL:
its fragrance is intense and persistent.

THERAPEUTIC PROPERTIES:
it is the calming oil par excellence (a few drops in the evening bath are enough to calm the liveliest child). It helps combat stress, insomnia, depression, palpitations, hysteria, and panic. It is indicated for all psychosomatic symptoms due to stress.

WARNING:
do not exceed the prescribed dose. Used in excessive doses, it can cause vomiting.

IT MIXES WELL WITH:
almost all oils, but particularly with geranium and lavender.

FOR MASSAGE:
dilute it in a basic oil by itself. With other essences, it is excellent for reducing stress.

OREGANO

The oil is obtained by distilling the whole plant, which grows in Europe.

BASIC OIL TONE:
the actual plant, from which the oil is obtained, is used in cooking for its aroma.

THERAPEUTIC PROPERTIES:
it is antiseptic, bactericidal, and antiviral.

WARNING:
do not use during pregnancy.

IT MIXES WELL WITH:
clove, rosemary, and sage.

FOR MASSAGE:
use oregano for aesthetic massage aimed at reducing cellulitis and fat deposits.

PEPPERMINT

This oil is distilled from the leaves and flowers of the plant. It is cultivated in Europe, the United States, and Japan. The English oil is considered the best.

MEDIUM OIL TONE: *because of its fragrance, it is also used in confectionary and in cosmetics.*

THERAPEUTIC PROPERTIES: *taken internally, it is a great substitute for aspirin. It fights diarrhea, car sickness, stomach aches, and flatulence. It is indicated for dysmenorrhea, skin inflammation, irritation,* *and insect bites. Useful against most weaknesses of the body, it is helpful for neuralgia, bronchitis, influenza, sinusitis, and headaches due to poor digestion.*

WARNING: *this oil can cause irritation, therefore remember to dilute it well.*

IT MIXES WELL WITH: *eucalyptus, marjoram, and rosemary.*

FOR MASSAGE: *peppermint works wonders for massage on the elderly since it increases body tone and soothes pain.*

PINE

The oil is obtained by distilling the leaves and branches of this widely grown plant.

SUPERIOR TONE OIL: *thanks to its fresh aroma, it is used to cleanse the air.*

THERAPEUTIC PROPERTIES: *it is antiseptic,* *anti-inflammatory, deodorizing, refreshing, and cures disorders in the respiratory tract.*

WARNING: *avoid using directly on the mucous membranes.*

IT MIXES WELL WITH: *bergamot, eucalyptus,* *and lemon.*

FOR MASSAGE: *thanks to its soothing and analgesic properties, this oil is useful in curative massage aimed at treating muscular pains and arthrosis.*

SAGE

Sage is a mediterranean plant whose oil is distilled from its leaves.

MEDIUM TONE OIL:
it is antiseptic, digestive, purifying, stimulating, diuretic, and disinfectant.

WARNING:
do not use during pregnancy. Do not exceed prescribed doses.

FOR MASSAGE:
it is excellent following a race, and for massage to prevent cramps.

ROSE

It is one of the most expensive and effective oils. It is obtained by distilling roses.

BASIC TONE OIL:
it has a delicate but long lasting perfume.

THERAPEUTIC PROPERTIES:
rose is suitable for all anxiety-related problems, such as insomnia, headaches, depression, and tension.

WARNING:
do not exceed prescribed doses, as it is a very delicate oil.

IT MIXES WELL WITH:
calendula, lavender, and orange.

FOR MASSAGE:
mixed with orange, it works wonders if used for antistress massage.

SANDALWOOD

This oil is extracted from the center of the trunk and the roots of the tree which mainly grows in India.

BASIC TONE OIL:
it has a warm and sensual fragrance and is often used in perfumes.

THERAPEUTIC PROPERTIES:
an antiseptic, sandalwood may be used to gargle and is helpful in cases of bladder infection, colitis, and skin irritation.

WARNING:
do not use it in a pure state on the body.

IT MIXES WELL WITH:
cypress, frankincense, jasmine, and rose.

FOR MASSAGE:
use it well diluted for face massage against acne.

YLANG YLANG

It is called "the flower of flowers" and is distilled from plants which are grown in tropical countries.

BASIC TONE OIL:
its perfume is reminiscent of jasmine.

THERAPEUTICAL PROPERTIES:
ylang ylang is considered relaxing and an aphrodisiac. It stimulates the production of adrenalin, tones up the heart, regulates the blood pressure, and is antiseptic.

WARNING:
excessive use can provoke headaches and nausea.

IT MIXES WELL WITH:
frankincense, jasmine, and sandalwood.

FOR MASSAGE:
this oil on its own, or mixed with other essences, is suitable for massages before a race.

GLOSSARY

ARTHRITIS

is a form of acute or chronic joint inflammation.
CLINICAL SYMPTOMS: swelling of the joint; it becomes hot, painful, reddened and impossible to move.
THERAPY: anti-inflammatory medicine, as prescribed by the doctor. Hot and cold compresses, inactivity. Swedish massage is not advised.
All reflexive therapies are effective.
EXAMPLES: frozen shoulder (the arm cannot be moved, even passively).

ARTHROSIS

is a chronic degenerative joint disease, caused by age and made worse by repeated traumas and by overweight.
CLINICAL SYMPTOMS: X-rays show a diminished consistency of the joint cartilage and the formation of apophysis (osteophyte). Pain is not always present. When moved, the joint "creaks". Movement is often limited.
THERAPY: heat in all its forms, Swedish massage, Shiatsu, passive mobilization.
Light physical activity.
EXAMPLES: knee, hip, cervical, and lumbar arthrosis.

CROOKED FOOT

is when the foot does not lean on the heel (club foot), or the foot is turned outwards (knock-kneed), is turned inwards (bandy-legged), or the foot is flexed and does not lean on the tip. These deformities are normally congenital.
CLINICAL SYMPOMS: as indicated above.
THERAPY: physical therapy.

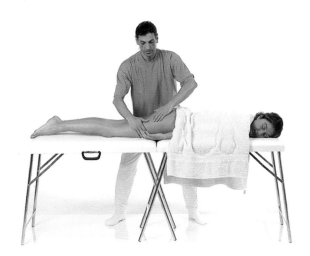

DISLOCATION

is the displacement of a bone from its natural position in the joint.
CLINICAL SYMPTOMS: the joint is swollen with signs of blood effusion. It is often accompanied by a pulled muscle.
THERAPY: a technique carried out by a specialist in order to return the joints to their proper place, connective tissue massage.

EDEMA

is an effusion of watery fluid into the connective tissue.
CLINICAL SYMPTOMS: a part of the body swells to a certain degree.
THERAPY: if the problem is due to water retention, lymphatic drainage may be performed.

EPICONDYLITIS

is the inflammation of the epicondyle, the bone protuberance of the elbow joint.
CLINICAL SYMPTOMS: pain and difficulty of movement.
THERAPY: rest, an immobilizing bandage, physical therapy (laser beams, radar therapy, ultrasounds).

FLAT FEET

is when the arches of the feet have fallen.
CLINICAL SYMPTOMS: the arch tends to touch the ground.
THERAPY: physical therapy, corrective gymnastics, and massage on the leg muscles and the lumbar-dorsal region.

GOUT

is a disorder of the smaller joints due to the body's difficulties in eliminating uric acid.
CLINICAL SYMPTOMS: acute pain triggered by fatigue or a heavy meal; reddening of the joint, edema.
THERAPY: pharmacological. Do not massage during the acute phase. Increase the intake of liquids, and perform draining and detoxifying massage during the chronic phase.

HEMATOMA

is a bruise caused by the clotting of blood following a vein burst.
CLINICAL SYMPTOMS: the area turns bluish.

THERAPY: pharmacological, as prescribed by the doctor. Massage may later help to free the damaged tissue from the adhesions caused by the healing process.

HYPERTENSION
is excessive increase in blood pressure.
CLINICAL SYMPTOMS: they are evaluated using the blood pressure gauge.
THERAPY: diuretics, as prescribed by the doctor. The increase in pressure is often due to stress. Therefore, antistress massage may be useful, after medical consultation.

HYPERTONIA
is excessive muscle tone.
CLINICAL SYMPTOMS: the muscle is hard and tight, reflexes are above standard.
THERAPY: relaxation, passive mobilization in hot water, Shiatsu.

HYPOTONIA
is inadequate muscle tone.
CLINICAL SYMPTOMS: the muscle is flaccid and weak.
THERAPY: electrostimulation, all types of massage.

LUMBAGO
is pain in the lumbar region.
CLINICAL SYMPTOMS: pain and stiffness.
THERAPY: stretching, all types of massage.

MONOPLEGIA
is when there is paralysis of a single limb or a single group of muscles.
CLINICAL SYMPTOMS: at onset of symptoms, flaccid

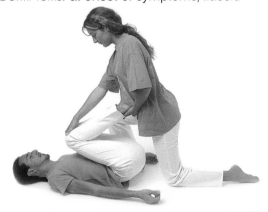

muscles and absence of reflexes. Later there is muscular spasticity and hyperreflexia.
THERAPY: physical therapy. In the second phase, very gentle stroking or Shiatsu.

MYATROPHY
is muscular wasting; the muscles lose volume and size.
CLINICAL SYMPTOMS: noticeable reduction in the muscular mass and loss of elasticity.
THERAPY: physical therapy (especially electrostimulation) and all types of massage.

MYOSITIS
is the inflammation of the muscle tissue.
CLINICAL SYMPTOMS: pain and localized edema.
THERAPY: pharmacological, inactivity, connective tissue massage, and Shiatsu carried out with the palm of the hand.

NEURITIS
is nerve inflammation.
CLINICAL SYMPTOMS: sensory and motor disorders, skin irritability along the nerve.
THERAPY: pharmacological, Shiatsu.

OSTEOPOROSIS
is a decrease of calcium in the bones.
CLINICAL SYMPTOMS: deep-seated pain, difficulty with certain movements.
THERAPY: pharmacological, preventive, isometric gymnastics, Swedish and connective tissue massage. Shiatsu is not advised.

PARAPLEGIA
is paralysis of the lower limbs.
CLINICAL SYMPTOMS: lower limbs are flaccid (hypotone) or more often spastic (hypertone).
THERAPY: physical therapy, connective tissue massage, Shiatsu.

PERIARTHRITIS
is inflammation of the tissues surrounding the joint.
CLINICAL SYMPTOMS: pain during movement.
THERAPY: inactivity, connective tissue massage, Shiatsu.
EXAMPLES: frozen shoulder.

PHLEBITIS

is vein inflammation, often caused by a clot (thrombophlebitis).

CLINICAL SYMPTOMS: it mainly affects the lower limbs, and manifests itself through widespread pain, high temperature, edema, and a volume increase of the groin lymph nodes.

THERAPY: it is mainly preventive. Manual lymphatic drainage helps eliminate the edema which remains after the acute phase is past.

POLYARTHRITIS

is inflammation of several joints. It may be chronic and progressive.

CLINICAL SYMPTOMS: acute pain attacks. Increase in the volume, reddening, and an effusion of blood in a joint, (particularly hands and elbows). Extreme difficulty of movement and ankylosis.

THERAPY: pharmacological (the disease evolves nonetheless).

POLYNEURITIS

is a generalized inflammation of the peripheral nerves.

CLINICAL SYMPTOMS: paralysis and sensory disorders.

THERAPY: the origin of the illness is treated (alcohol and diabetes). It is possible to treat with Shiatsu.

POLYRADICOLONEURITIS

is also called the syndrome Guyllain Barrè and is an inflammation of the roots of several peripheral nerves.

CLINICAL SYMPTOMS: flaccid paralysis, the muscles lose tone, sensitivity disorders.

THERAPY: anti-inflammatory medicine as prescribed by a doctor. Shiatsu may improve muscle tone.

PULLED MUSCLES

occur when there has been an overstepping of the elasticity threshold due to an abrupt movement or excessive physical strain.

CLINICAL SYMPTOMS: at the moment of injury, an acute pain is felt; it is impossible to contract the muscle. There is an increase in blood effusion.

THERAPY: inactivity with bandages and the application of anti-edema creams. At the end of the inactivity period, Swedish massage should be applied to reactivate circulation and bring the muscle back to its normal activity.

RADICULITIS

is an inflammation of the nerve roots of the vertebral column.

CLINICAL SYMPTOMS: paresis (partial paralysis), disorders of sensitivity, skin irritability.

THERAPY: anti-inflammatory medicine (as prescribed by a doctor), connective tissue massage, Shiatsu.

SACRALIZATION

is a tendency of the fifth lumbar vertebra to adhere to the sacrum.

CLINICAL SYMPTOMS: lumbo-sacral pain, decreased joint range of motion, and muscle stiffness.

THERAPY: specific gymnastics (analgesic and corrective), Swedish and corrective tissue massage, and Shiatsu.

SCIATICA

is widespread pain in the sciatic nerve area.

CLINICAL SYMPTOMS: pain in the buttocks, in the lumbar area, in the thigh, and in the leg.

THERAPY: depending on the cause of pain–traction, Swedish massage, connective tissue massage, Shiatsu, reflexology may be carried out. During the acute phase, rest is advised.

SCOLIOSIS

is a lateral curvature of the spine. There is often a secondary curve to compensate for the first.

CLINICAL SYMPTOMS: the curve can be observed both through X-rays and with the naked eye. The paravertebral muscles develop asymetrically.

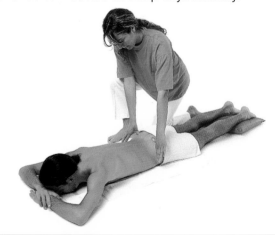

THERAPY: corrective stretching and muscular development; massage, where there is pain.

SPRAIN

is a straining or twisting of the ligaments or muscles of a joint, of traumatic origin. Often caused by a faulty movement of the joints.
CLINICAL SYMPTOMS: the joint becomes swollen with blood effusion and edema, painful and hot.
THERAPY: anti-edema cream, light bandaging, inactivity.

STIFF NECK

is caused by prolonged twisting of the neck, often associated with spasms of the breastbone.
CLINICAL SYMPTOMS: pain in the neck, the head cannot be moved without pain.
THERAPY: hot compresses, massage with camphor-based cream. In extreme cases, wearing a cervical collar is advised.

STRETCH MARKS

are scar tissue, deriving from elastic skin tissue giving way.
CLINICAL SYMPTOMS: they appear as long scars, at first red, then fairly white.
THERAPY: they can only be prevented by a suitable diet, cosmetic products with an elasticine base, massage, and physical activity.

SYNOVITIS

is inflammation of a synovial membrane.
CLINICAL SYMPTOMS: severe pain in a joint.
THERAPY: anti-inflammatory medicines (as prescribed by a doctor). Muscular support through the use of wrist and ankle bands.
EXAMPLES: carpal tunnel syndrome.

TENDINITIS

is an inflammation of a tendon caused by repeated small injuries.

CLINICAL SYMPTOMS: localized pain, with extreme difficulty in contracting the corresponding muscle.
THERAPY: anti-inflammatory medicine (as prescribed by a doctor), inactivity, rest.
EXAMPLES: inflammation of Achilles tendon in runners.

THROMBOPHLEBITIS

is the formation of blood clots on the inner walls of the veins.
CLINICAL SYMPTOMS: pains in the lower limbs, especially in the calf; high temperature, swelling of the groin lymph glands. Varicose veins and edema can occur later.
THERAPY: anti-inflammatory medicines, as prescribed by a doctor. Massage must on no account be performed. After the acute phase, it may be useful to practice lymphatic drainage to drain the edema and empty the lymph nodes.

VALGUS

is a term which means bent outward or twisted, and generally applies to the foot or knee.
CLINICAL SYMPTOMS: external rotation of the foot or the knee, often combined with flat feet. Pain or difficulty while walking.
THERAPY: corrective gymnastics. Massage helps to calm the pain.

VARUS

is a term which means turned inward, and usually applies to the foot or knee.
CLINICAL SYMPTOMS: curved legs, typical of cowboys.
THERAPY: corrective gymnastics, Swedish massage, and foot reflexogy to alleviate the muscle pain associated with this condition.

INDEX